Ask the Pastor

Ask the Pastor

Practical Answers
to Your Questions
About Life and Faith

Pastor Gary Mortara

with Shea Gregory

ISBN: 978-0692343845

For Cricket

Your faith has sparked untold journeys.

For the Faith Fellowship Family

Continue to grow in the things of God.

Acknowledgments

I wish to express my deepest appreciation to my beautiful and amazing wife, Tisha. Your constant support and encouragement allow me to soar. Thank you, always.

Special thanks to the many individuals who have made this book possible:

To the Faith Fellowship Wednesday night Bible study family. Your willingness to ask questions, and your desire to grow spiritually formed the foundation for this book. Keep seeking Him.

Thank you to Merry Montgomery and Kelly Scott for assistance with the rough draft; and to Pastor Raul Rico for seeing the project through to the end.

A very special thank you to Sandy King for your tireless review of the manuscript for jargon, jots, tittles, flaws, and everything in between. Your labor of love has not been in vain. May the Lord bless your efforts above and beyond what you've ever imagined.

Contents

Introduction

I am blessed to pastor a life-giving church in Northern California, right in the heart of the San Francisco Bay Area. Our community is a thriving metropolis of nine million people with a demographic as diverse as the landscape. Within our congregation, we have an awesome mix of cultures and backgrounds. It is the coolest church in the world to pastor.

A few years ago, a woman came up to me and said, "I have so many questions to ask you about life and the Bible. When and where can I do that? I can't make an appointment to see you every time I have a question." As I quickly thought about her comments, I responded by saying, "Why don't you write your questions down on a piece of paper, and I'll answer them during Bible study." Little did I know that this practice would quickly be adopted by others and become a regular part of our mid-week Bible study.

Each week, this Q and A session adds a little flair to our service and usually provides some humor and thought provoking insights. We answer just about everything you can think of (and some questions you probably haven't or wouldn't dare to ask in church). Topics range from the second coming of Christ, all they way to intimacy in marriage, and just about everything in between. You name it, we've probably heard it! The questions are all asked anonymously but answered in front of everyone.

This book is a compilation of some of those questions concerning the Bible and life's issues. It will provide you with biblical theology as well as answers to questions you may not have thought to ask. My prayer is that these questions and answers will encourage your faith, spark conversations, and lead you to deeper study of the Word.

And if you ever have a question for me to answer, just write it down and *ASK THE PASTOR.*

Blessings on you,
Pastor Gary

CHAPTER 1

Catholicism

My daughter and her family are Catholics. Would it be all right to attend their church services for special occasions?

Absolutely. Of course you can attend, just like Catholics are welcome to attend our services. If you attend a Catholic service, you are not going to be harmed by it in any way. The Catholic Church holds to certain doctrines that we, as Protestants, do not agree with or believe. Go ahead and go with your daughter and her family and enjoy your time together. If you have questions, ask them in a non-threatening, non-accusing way and listen without trying to force your views on anyone. When the opportunity presents itself to share your differences, show them what the Bible says. Be respectful and let the Word convict them. You must continue to read and study your Bible. You need to be grounded in biblical doctrine, so you are not swayed by the extra-biblical, religious teachings and traditions of the Catholic Church.

Pastor, my family, is having a hard time getting used to my leaving the Catholic Church and coming to Faith Fellowship and accepting Jesus Christ as Lord and Savior. I haven't told everyone in my family except for a few close relatives.

Your movement toward a Spirit-filled, Bible teaching, Protestant church body doesn't have to be a splitting from the Catholic Church as though Catholicism is something bad. Catholics believe in the same Jesus Christ.

Let your family know that you believe in the same Lord and Savior. You are not chasing after a foreign god, nor have you renounced your faith. Ask them, "What is a Christian?" A Christian is a believer in Jesus as Lord and Savior. Jesus is the Son of God. He was born of a virgin. He lived a sinless life. He died on a cross for our sins. He rose from the dead and ascended to Heaven. He will come again as the reigning King. So, whether you go to the Catholic Church or the Protestant Church, as long as you believe in the Lord Jesus Christ, the sinless and eternal Son of God, you are a Christian

That being said, at the appropriate time, you can let your family know that there are some beliefs and practices that you will no longer observe because the two denominations disagree on these issues. There are traditions and beliefs within the Catholic Church that have no biblical basis and we, as Protestants, do not practice them. Let your loved ones know that you are not trying to offend them and remind them that you are not moving away from God. If anything, you are moving closer to God. Use the Bible to show your differences.

You will be learning things at Faith Fellowship that you did not learn in the Catholic Church. Unfortunately, there are many Catholics (and Protestants!) who are not saved and do not know **biblically** how to get saved. This is very heart wrenching. The biblical truth is that Jesus is the only Savior – not Mary nor the Mass nor anything else.

Let your faith and your Christ-like attitude be a witness to your family. Ask them not to reject you because you are moving closer to the Lord. Remember that if your family members have been deeply rooted in the Catholic tradition, they will have a very difficult time with your separation from their belief system. They may think you are jeopardizing your chances of getting into heaven. Recognize that their fear is because they love you, and they want what they believe is best for you. Continue to love them. Listen, but do not argue. Learn all you can about the Word of God, so you can rightly understand practices, traditions, and truth.

***How can we convince Catholics that Jesus is more important
than Mary? Mary had her purpose, but Jesus shed the blood.***

If you look at the historical research, you can get an understanding
of Catholics, their stance regarding Mary, and why they elevate her
to the position of co-redemtrix with Christ.

Basically, you have to know your Bible. In 1Timothy 2:5,
the Bible says, "For there is one God and one mediator between
God and mankind, the man Christ Jesus." You are right. Jesus is
the One who shed his blood, and Jesus clearly stated, "I am the
way and the truth and the life. No one comes to the Father except
through me" (John 14: 6).

Catholics will begin to defend their points with tradition –
things taught by the church, by the leadership, and by the Pope
and others down through the years who say Mary was
immaculately conceived. They say that when her parents
conceived her, she was not born in sin. It is an argument they will
go around and around with you about. They will say Mary was
perpetually a virgin – that she never had physical intimacy with her
husband, even though the Bible says that she had other sons and
daughters. Their argument simply does not stand up to the test of
Scripture.

Approach conversations about faith using the Bible as
your plumb line. Speak in love, not accusingly, not pontificating,
and not condemning. Again, speak in love. As you share the truth

of Scripture, pray and trust that the Holy Spirit will reveal truth to hearts and minds. So, even though it's not your job to convince anyone, it is your job to know the Word and to be able to defend your faith and the truth of Scripture against unbiblical teachings.

I have a friend who is not saved. He is a good man and is going through many trials. He has started attending a Catholic church and is not willing to come to our church at this time. Should I discourage him from going to the Catholic Church?

No, do not discourage him. He is hearing the Word of God. Be his friend and encourage him to continue going to church. Pray for him and continue to live out your faith. You are aware of the differences between our doctrine and the doctrine of the Catholic Church.

What you could do is tell him that you will visit his church, and you would like him to visit yours. If he is not saved, do not let your heart fall for him just because you feel sorry for him. He may be steeped in Catholicism and may also be very religious, but that does not mean that he is saved. You must guard your heart and direct him to a pastor or Christian counselor who can encourage him and walk with him through this difficult season in his life.

In your view, why would someone convert from being Protestant to being Catholic? I have a friend who was Protestant for many years and is now an avowed Catholic.

This is an interesting question because about half of our church converted from Catholicism to Protestantism. It is a bit less frequent to find people moving from being Protestant to being Catholic. If they do, the main reasons may be because they really like the structure and the practices of Catholicism. Think about it, there is a sense of security in structure, routine, and being given exactly what to repeat, say, and pray. Catholicism is very well organized. Whichever Catholic church you go to on a given Saturday or Sunday, whether you are in the USA, Latin America, Europe or Canada, each is reading from the same text; each is going through the same liturgy. They are all in one accord.

Perhaps your friend feels that the Catholic services are more reverent than ours are in the Protestant church. Sometimes this construction attracts people. However, we do believe that the Word of God is taught at a deeper level in many Protestant churches (although not all).

Usually, in a Catholic church, you are not going to have the kind of worship that you have in a Protestant church. In a Catholic service, everyone is participating and acting in unison (the standing, the sitting, the kneeling, as well as the congregational responses, and so on). As a religious system, this attracts some people. The Catholic Church, however, holds to quite a few traditions and customs that we do not follow.

We believe in the same God, the same Lord Jesus, the same Holy Spirit, and the same Bible (to an extent). There are, however, some teachings within the Catholic belief system that we, as Protestants, do not believe (or practice) – for example, the mass, ideas regarding Mary, reciting the rosary, doing penance, praying to saints, and doctrinal issues concerning eternal life.

Overall, I think if your friend had been Protestant and converted to Catholicism, he or she was probably attracted by the structure and the sense of reverence for God that can sometimes be lacking in our Protestant churches.

Is a believer of faith in Catholicism considered evenly yoked with a Protestant believer?

If a Catholic believer has faith in the Lord Jesus Christ, yes, the two would be evenly yoked. However, a believer in the "faith of Catholicism" would be someone who believes only in a religious system. As Protestants, we do not agree with many of Catholicism's doctrines and practices. They oblige people to adhere to extra-biblical requirements that we do not accept as biblically sound, and there are some vast differences between Protestant and Catholic theology. At the same time, we know that there will be Catholics in heaven along with many Protestants. People from one group who love the Lord Jesus Christ and have accepted him as Savior, have repented of their sins, and are trying to live their lives in a pleasing way are just as saved as those from the other group.

Would I recommend that a Protestant Christian marry a Catholic? It depends. Would I be okay with a Protestant Christian marrying a Catholic who has accepted Jesus Christ as his or her Lord and Savior, who reads the Bible, and who practices the Word of God? Yes, I would.

What is the rosary?

The term "rosary" comes from the Latin for "a garland of roses." The rose is a symbol of Mary, whom Catholics believe to be a perpetual virgin. The rosary is a set of prayer reminders. Each bead is a prayer – The Lord's Prayer, the Apostle's Creed, and so on. There is also the Hail Mary: *Hail Mary, full of grace. The Lord is with thee. Blessed art thou amongst women, and blessed is the fruit of thy womb, Jesus. Holy Mary, Mother of God, pray for us sinners, now and at the hour of our death. Amen.*

The beads serve as reminders for specific prayers – some of which are from the Word of God. Catholics would say that the other prayers, although not directly from the Word, do not contradict the Word. We would disagree with that.

Like with any prayer, there is a problem when it becomes a perfunctory, habitual, "not even thinking about it" kind of prayer. When it becomes that, then what are we doing? If we are simply mechanically repeating phrases, is that really prayer? That's not what God is looking for. He would rather have ten words of our heartfelt expression than mindless repetitions of meaningless phrases.

The main thing is that when you pray, you don't want to fall into habitual, rote prayers that end up meaning nothing to you. Jesus said that even the pagans go on and on mumbling, thinking their many words will be heard by God. But God is not interested in that kind of prayer. God is looking for prayer that is from the heart.

The rosary can serve to focus one's prayers, or it can become a tool to get through your prayers without having to think much about what you are saying.

CHAPTER 2

Christian Living, Practice, and Traditions

When Christians are talking negatively about other Christians, how do I excuse myself from the situation or interject with positive things?

You just gave us two very good options. You can excuse yourself from the conversation, or you can interject positive things. You can also be overt and say, "Aren't we believers? We shouldn't be talking about that person that way." Keep a straight face when you say it. They will think twice about speaking negatively about others in front of you next time and, hopefully, will begin to examine their hearts and recognize their sin.

Is it a sin or wrong to teach kids about Santa Claus, the Easter Bunny, or the Tooth Fairy?

I personally don't see the harm when your children are little. Up to age five or so it's probably fine but, at some point, you just need to come clean. A lot of kids figure it out, some before others. After a certain age, they must be told the truth. More importantly, make sure they understand what specific holidays are really about.

Is it wrong to participate in secular holidays such as Halloween?

If your children are old enough, make sure they know the meanings behind the holidays and why people celebrate them. For us, Halloween is not a holiday. We have a Harvest Festival in place of Halloween. We make it a celebration with a Christian theme and have a great time. We do this in place of the secular celebration. If you want your kids to go trick-or-treating and things like that, it is totally up to you, but you (and they) should know what they are celebrating and make a conscious choice based on knowledge and information. Some people will feel that you should not be involved in some celebrations, while others will feel that participation is no big deal. You have to make a prayerful and educated decision for you and your family and extend grace to those who feel differently than you do.

Every year, my neighbor says I should not have a Christmas tree because it's a pagan ritual. My family loves having a tree. Are we wrong?

Whenever believers observe any holiday, we must look at why we are doing so, and what it means to us. For us, Christmas is an exciting time of celebration of the birth of our Lord and Savior Jesus Christ. The modern day Christmas tree is not pagan unless, of course, you are pagan and it is an idol in your home. We are not venerating trees or praying to them. If a Christian did celebrate with a Christmas tree as pagan tree worshipers once worshiped trees, then that would be a problem.

A tree brings you no closer to God, nor does it push you farther away. Putting up a Christmas tree does not mean you are observing a pagan ritual or paying homage to a pagan god. We are celebrating the Lord's virgin birth – a miracle of Almighty God. For many, having a Christmas tree is part of the tradition of the celebration. Whether or not you choose to have one is up to you.

Jeremiah 10:1-10 and Isaiah 44:14-19 (verses individuals sometimes use to decry the Christmas tree tradition) have nothing to do with the Christmas tree and everything to do with worshiping idols. Unless you are falling down before your Christmas tree and worshiping it, you're okay. Something to think about – perhaps the real idol is the materialism we have accepted as part of our Christmas tradition. Even Christians have fallen prey to overspending and focusing too much on purchasing sale items and giving each other gifts rather than focusing on the true meaning and glory of the season.

Is it okay for Christians to do yoga if the teacher is a Christian?

There are different kinds of yoga. There is the physical form that is basically stretching and exercise, and that's good for you. On the other hand, there is the yoga that involves deeper components of Eastern meditation tradition, and I would advise you to stay away from that form because you open yourself up to the belief system, practice, and all that is behind it.

Is it okay for a Christian to serve jury duty?

Absolutely, yes, it is fine for a Christian to serve jury duty. We are to live as responsible citizens, so there is nothing wrong with serving jury duty.

There is an orange tree in my neighbors' yard. I am okay with picking the fruit on my side of the fence. Is it okay to pick the fruit on their side of the fence? They cannot harvest the fruit that is against the fence, and it just falls to the ground. Am I stealing? Should I just ask my neighbor if it is okay to take the fruit?

It is always right and best to ask first. If you are on good terms, they will most likely tell you help yourself. If you aren't that close with them, this could be an icebreaker. You could ask, "Hey, the fruit is falling on your side and it's going to the ground wasted. Can I pick it up and give it to you?" Try to look for opportunities to let your light shine before others and glorify your Father in heaven (Matthew 5:16).

Can you teach about eating healthy, and tell us who did so in the Bible?

I talk about this in my book *Be A Man.* The Old Testament teaches dietary laws that we don't much live by anymore. The Jewish dietary laws were extremely healthy. They ate natural grains, fruits, vegetables, and lean meat.

It goes without saying that we don't eat well in this country, and many of us do not exercise. Some people are simply unaware of the kinds of foods that cause the body to put on extra pounds (including sugary soft drinks). If you want to make a change, start today. Get educated on what's good for your body and what's not. Talk to your doctor or a health professional and get some good nutritional advice. Once you've done that, get a partner; find someone to pray with you, someone who will help keep you accountable as you begin your journey to a healthier you.

For some, nutritional knowledge is enough to begin making sustainable changes in long-term health and nutrition. For others, knowledge itself will never be enough. They know they should not eat as much as they do, but the challenge to change is just too difficult. Some people believe that folks who have eating problems simply lack basic self-discipline, but this lack of self control is usually rooted in deeper issues. The excess eating is a symptom of something that is going on at a deeper, subconscious level. Many people have long held patterns of thinking and behaving that cause them to turn to food when they are not really hungry. At some point in life, these dear brothers and sisters began turning to food for comfort or to escape difficult emotions. As much as they try, they are unable to stop the compulsion to overeat.

Some people will exercise and exercise, run on the treadmill, and practice all kinds of seemingly positive behaviors. They will eat small plates of food when they are around other people. But once they get alone, and no one is looking, it's a different story. They splurge and eat foods loaded with unhealthy carbohydrates and far too much sugar. They overindulge on portions that are too large for one individual. When they are all alone, that's when they cannot control themselves.

If you recognize yourself in any of what I just said, it's time to go to *Celebrate Recovery* or *Overeaters Anonymous*. It's time to begin to heal from habits that are keeping you stuck in unhealthy eating patterns. God wants to do some healing in your body and in your mind. He wants to reveal the hurt behind the symptoms of overeating. Can you trust Him enough to get help? He wants to fill those unfilled, hurting places that are making you think you need more salt, more fat, and more sugar to fill the emptiness inside you.

Everyone can become a healthy eater, but some will need more help and guidance than others.

In the Old Testament, it states what you can and cannot eat. If eating pork was a sin, and if the Israelites also weren't supposed to eat anything from the sea that didn't have scales, does that mean that it's sin to eat those things now?

No, it is not a sin to eat those things now. In Mark 7, Jesus states that it is not what goes into a man that makes him unclean, but it's what comes out of a man that makes him unclean (Mark 7:18-22). Mark comments that, by this, Jesus was declaring all foods clean. "Clean" meant ceremonially clean. This meant the Israelites could approach God. God had restricted the Jews from eating certain foods so they would remain ceremonially clean. Actually, the prohibited foods mentioned in the Old Testament have been medically proven to be harmful to you. However, it doesn't mean that you are cut off from God or that it's a sin if you eat them today. They're just not particularly healthy for you.

The Jews were God's holy, separated, and consecrated people, and God wanted them to live a certain way. He gave them laws of the physical body: *You are to work six days.* He gave them dietary laws: *You are to eat certain foods and abstain from certain foods.* He ordered them to rest: *You are to rest one day a week.* And so by exercise, diet, and rest, a healthy body is maintained.

But as far as being religiously or ceremonially clean, those are not dietary restrictions that you have to adhere to as a believer. However, if you continue to eat some of the junk food you are eating, you are probably going to die prematurely. Your food intake does matter, and you want to be mindful of it.

My husband and I have a disagreement regarding our children's future and the issue of being or not being equally yoked. When our kids are sixteen, we will allow them to date. I want to make it a rule that they can only date Christians until they are old enough to make their own choices (around age eighteen), but my husband doesn't think it's right and that it will only cause conflict. What do you suggest?

Dating is one of the most serious things a teenager is going to do as a teenager. If my daughter (or your daughter) could not show responsibility in some of the lesser important things in life, what in the world would make her think I would allow her to date? You and I both know what it is like to be a teenager. How many of us remember being teenagers?

Let me talk to the guys for a moment. Men, how did we act when we knocked on a young lady's door and her parents answered? We were so polite, weren't we? "Good evening Mrs. Johnson, you look so lovely today. Is that a new hair style? It looks so good on you. Hello Mr. Johnson, nice lawn you've got there. Can I help you with anything around the house? Do you need me to take out the trash?"

Then you drove off in the car with the young lady, and you behaved like a leech and a parasite out for blood.

I would not let your daughter date until she is showing an appropriate level of maturity and responsibility. Let's be honest; kids are human beings. When a kiss starts, or when a touch starts, it is nearly impossible to stop. Why would any of us want to put our children in that situation? Christian boy or non-Christian – being saved won't make a difference. I'm sorry to have to say that. Not until there is a "mature" level of responsibility being shown by your daughter would I let her be alone with a boy. It's best not to allow something to happen that she may later regret. My daughter might be thirty-one before I let her go out alone with a guy. I'm kidding, of course, but you get the point.

Ladies, do some of you wish your daddies had taken a more proactive role regarding the young men in your life? Remember some of the bums you went out with?

Is it okay to dedicate an infant if the parents are not married yet?

First, we would meet and talk with the parents and make sure they truly understand what it is we are doing. It is not simply a religious thing; it is a Christian thing, a spiritual thing. It is done in faith and in all seriousness. We would endeavor to show the parents that we are asking God to watch over their child's life. First and foremost, we would encourage the couple to get married. We would let them know we are also dedicating them as parents to raising their child in the ways of the Lord. If they don't want to accept that, we may still dedicate the child to the Lord. That does make it a paradox for the parents, though. They want the child to serve the Lord but refuse to do so themselves? The situation would create a confusing family dynamic.

So, to answer the question – possibly. We are praying God's covering and protection and blessing over the child. God loves little children. Jesus said, "Let the little children come to me, and do not hinder them, for the kingdom of God belongs to such as these" (Mark 10:14, Matthew 19:14).

During the dedication service, parents are also making a commitment to raise the child in a godly manner.

I go to school with a lot of people who curse. I'm getting a little freaked out because their words are going around in my head; how can I forget them?

Well, you could ask the people you are hanging out with not to curse so much around you. That would be very bold of you. Be warned – if you take such a stance, you will be challenged.

I wonder if you are feeling a bit of pressure to be with these people. Peer pressure can be very difficult to escape, especially if you are young. At the same time, you have a responsibility to yourself. If you recognize yourself going in the wrong direction, who is the one person who can make you turn around and go differently? You.

One exercise you can daily practice is to fill your mind with God's Word. Are you regularly reading your Bible? Are you memorizing Scripture? Are you spending some time alone each day with the Lord? When those thoughts that are contrary to God's best for you come into your head, confront them with the truth of God's Word. But to do this, you must know what the Word says.

If this group of friends is having a negative influence on you, could you gradually separate yourself from them and begin hanging out with people who don't curse so much? Begin praying and asking God to direct you toward people who love Him. Ask Him to open doors of new friendships with other believers. Be open to meeting new people and making some changes regarding who you hang out with. It's not that you have to shun your old crowd (unless of course you are being pulled back to your old ways), but you can begin to form new relationships with people who are moving in the same direction you are. You will gain strength from other believers and will have a bit more mental muscle power when you do hang around the old crowd.

Take a look at 2 Timothy 2:22. Paul instructs Timothy to flee the evil desires of youth and pursue righteousness, faith, love and peace along with those who call on the Lord out of a pure heart. In the same way, you must take the courageous route. Be an influencer of men and not the one being led astray.

I heard someone say that beauty is a leader. What does that mean? What about those of us who are simply average looking?

Women admire other women who are wise, confident, and sensitive. If you throw beauty in the mix, then you have a woman that other women will follow.

When a woman carries herself in a godly way, speaks with wisdom, shows confidence, is sensitive to others, and is beautiful in attitude and in how she takes care of herself, women will listen to her. However, outer physical beauty is only one ingredient in the recipe. An "average" looking woman (according to the world's or a society's definition of beauty) with the beauty of Christ shining through her eyes and evident in her lifestyle is a true jewel. Other women will be attracted to her and will want to learn from her. Physical beauty is always overshadowed by one's heart and deeds in the long run. Physical beauty is just one factor of who a woman is, and it's definitely not the most important.

Is talking on the cell phone while driving a sin?

Well, technically, sin is defined as transgression of a law. What is the purpose of laws? They are there to protect you and to protect others. Should you be talking on a hand held phone while driving? Should you be texting while driving? No, you should not. So, technically, yes, it is a sin. Murder is also a sin. Am I saying that the two are equal? No, but sin is sin. Could your disobeying the law cause potential harm to yourself or to someone else? Definitely. So pull over and handle your business.

Think about it. There was a time when we had to wait to talk to someone. We waited until we got home, or we found a pay phone. Modern technology is wonderful, but has it become our master? That may sound extreme, but consider it for a few minutes.

I need some advice about what to do. I used to live with my sister, and I put my name on her lease to make her rent cheaper. We had a falling out and I moved away, but I left my name on the lease to still help her out, even though she stole money from me and lied about it. I have since forgiven her for what she has done. Now, however, she hasn't paid her rent and is getting evicted. My name is still on her lease, and her landlord is taking me to court to get the past due rent. I don't talk to my sister anymore, and I cannot get a place to live because of the situation. Any advice on what I can do? I forgave her once, and this situation has made it very difficult for me.

Unfortunately, you will have to pay the tab for this debt. You had the wrong motive for signing on the lease in the first place. Sometimes by "helping" we are actually enabling. Enabling is not grace, and it is not love. Enabling makes it possible for someone to continue in the same destructive patterns she or he has become accustomed to. We do it because we often don't have the courage to take a firm stance that sets a person on the right course.

Your sister later stole from you, but you left your name on the lease? Was that a loving act? She seems to have a pattern of bad and irresponsible behavior. Were you expecting her to behave differently this time? Was your supporting her ongoing bad habits acting in her best interest?

Never, ever co-sign for anybody, ever. Even if you co-sign for someone you feel you really know, it puts the relationship in a funny place, and there are going to be weird feelings between you. The Book of Proverbs (6:1-5, 20:16, 22:26-27) warns us against co-signing, especially for strangers and wayward women. You fill in the definition of wayward.

You are accountable and responsible for the debt.

You ask about forgiveness. Remember that we are not to forgive just once. At the same time, that does not mean that you allow the person who hurt you access to harm you over and over again. We have a teaching from Matthew 18 on forgiveness. It is available on CD.

I encourage you to try to work it out with your sister. Humble yourself and sit down and talk with her. I think that by now you know not to ever loan her money or trust her with your things. You will have to use wisdom in setting boundaries with her, and you will have to use wisdom in knowing what kind of relationship to have with her.

How do you overcome stumbling blocks like addictions and bad habits? I'm sick and tired of myself. What is the key?

Celebrate Recovery (*CR*) is a ministry that helps folks deal with hurts, hang-ups, and habits. It is a nationwide organization, and you can look them up and find a meeting in your local area. You will get help and support, and I strongly encourage you to make a commitment to attend. *CR* meets here at our church on Monday nights.

Accountability is one of the keys to wholeness. You need accountability with others who will listen, encourage, and call you out regarding your stuff. You also must begin to learn to submit to the Holy Spirit. The Bible says that if you walk in the Spirit, you will not fulfill the lusts of the flesh. You learn to walk in obedience to God's Word by the Holy Spirit's power and by being honest with God, with yourself, and with others.

Often people abuse themselves to fill a void. Maybe you know what that void is, but maybe you do not. Have you ever gotten any counseling? Sometimes extra help is necessary to work through the hurts of the past. Once addictions form, deep patterns of thinking and behavior have formed in the brain, and you are not able to change on your own.

Changing your actions begins with changing your thinking. Being in church, reading your Bible, seeking counsel – all of these will help you begin thinking and acting differently.

Are you willing to be honest with yourself and admit that you need help and that you cannot do it on your own? If so, this admission of powerlessness is the first step in the recovery process. Many of us want a quick fix – a key that unlocks an imaginary door to wholeness. It took time for you to get messed up; it's going to take some time for you to get whole. Are you willing to invest the time to allow yourself to heal? If so, begin now by looking up some local meetings such as CR (*Celebrate*

Recovery), AA (*Alcoholics Anonymous*), NA (*Narcotics Anonymous*), OA (*Overeaters Anonymous*), SAA (*Sex Addicts Anonymous*), or whatever the need might be. If you are really serious, go this week; go today. Take the first steps toward healing.

How do you keep your faith when you are out in the world? I play worship music all the time, but I still get angry and frustrated trying to get my kids out of the house in the morning or while driving in traffic.

I'll be honest with you; you are not alone in this challenge. Keeping your faith and keeping your cool are common struggles for most believers. It sounds like you have developed a habit with the kids in the morning, so let's think of another way to handle your morning routine. What *can* you do differently? Some preplanning is necessary. How could you re-work your morning so that you are not rushing everyone out of the house, and you are not running around like "crazy mom"?

Begin to think ahead. One thing you can do is mentally prepare yourself. Think of how you can act differently in those situations where you usually get all worked up and lose your cool. You know the daily routines that cause you the most stress, and you know the types of circumstances that irritate and frustrate you. There is nothing wrong with getting frustrated. The Bible says it's okay to be frustrated. You may be frustrated but do not sin. If your emotions are getting the best of you to where you cannot help yourself, then you are letting your flesh override your spirit. You are not exercising self control.

Think about how you are going to deal with the morning issues and what you can do to alleviate the morning tension. Help your children have a morning that is not anxious and full of stress. How are you going to speak and act? How do you want to sound and appear as a mom and as a godly woman? How do you want to behave?

Take responsibility and begin with small changes in your morning schedule (and your evening preparation for the next day). Start new habits, however small they may seem at first, and then grow from there.

If you are leaving the house late and then are frustrated because other drivers are not speeding along, you have to take a step back and realize that if you left the house on time (or early), you would not be so upset with others on the road.

If you find yourself getting frustrated a lot, maybe you need to take a closer look at your own personal issues. There are people who seem to be constantly frustrated with and offended by others. If that is the case, perhaps you should ask the Lord to begin to show you some things about yourself and ask Him to help you to grow into a more mature Christian, so you are not so easily angered and upset all the time. Practice being thankful.

I have an issue with someone at work and have spoken with HR. HR has advised me to speak with the person directly, but I know the person will get offended if I talk with her. How should I move forward if this issue continues? I want to keep peace.

You must do your part and be mature by approaching the person and appropriately addressing the issue. Talk to one of the elders or one of the pastors. Someone with more experience can help you figure out how to word your concern and how to make your approach. You are not responsible for how the person responds. If you have handled it properly, but your co-worker still gets offended, then you might have to take it back to HR. Let them know that you tried, but the person did not accept it. At that point, let HR help you.

We started reading the Bible with our six year old daughter. Please recommend a good children's Bible for me to read to her.

There are so many out there. Take a trip to your local Christian bookstore and peruse the children's Bibles and find the one that is best for you and your family. Also, check with some other families in the church who have children around the same age.

I was looking through all my secular music yesterday. I have not listened to it in a long time, but I was fondly remembering some of my favorite songs on those CD's. Is it necessary to stop listening to secular music, or is it okay to listen in moderation? Nowadays, I just listen to my praise and worship music.

It's a great and fair question. Many of the older songs, and even some modern ones, are not right or wrong, not good or bad; they're just music – they're simply amoral. Since you have gotten off to a great start by listening to praise and worship, I would encourage you not to turn back. If you do decide that you want to listen to some "good ole music" every once in a while, be mindful. If it begins to take up your time and your thinking and causes you to want to buy more new secular music that takes up more of your time, or if you begin to get entangled and start to lose the praise and worship that is in your heart – then I would encourage you to leave it alone. There is nothing wrong with listening to a good song. There is absolutely nothing wrong with it, but keep your praise on.

Why is it so hard to stop listening to secular music?

The enemy still has a hook in you – that's the bottom line. Now, some secular music is amoral. It's not good or bad, not right or wrong. You must realistically evaluate whether secular music has too high a place in your life. When you get in the car and all your stations are set to secular stations, you might ask yourself whether worldly music still has a hold on you. When you just *have to* listen to secular music, and you get emotionally tied to lyrics and phrases that are not God-honoring, then you have an issue to deal with because your heart is not fully given over to the Lord. That may be hard to admit because we like to convince ourselves that secular music is harmless. Carefully consider the messages you are continually putting in your mind.

It's very difficult to be a worshiping Christian when you are constantly listening to music that is contrary to the Word of God. What you put into your mind is what you will dwell on. You need to make a decision. What if you take a stance? What if you said, "Lord, for one month, I am not going to listen to secular music. I am going to listen to worship music for the next thirty days." Do it and see what happens in your life. See how your thinking changes.

There is so much good Christian music out there – a lot of it. You cannot say it all sounds too bland or too old fashioned. There is Christian music for whatever your taste might be.

When you ask God to thwart any plans that are not His will, does He do it?

There are Scriptures that recount times when people of God prayed this type of prayer, and God answered them accordingly. I cannot say that God ALWAYS does it. We each have free will to make decisions, good or bad, and our free will plays a definite part in our lives. God allows us to choose, even if it is against His will, and the consequences of a choice must run their course.

His perfect will was given in the Ten Commandments and yet, by acts of human free will, His perfect will is constantly violated.

If we really begin to intercede for people much more than we do, I think we would be surprised as to how many situations WOULD turn around. Prayer can be extremely effective – if we would just pray!

Does God interfere with court trials to make His will take place?

That depends on God. How many of you should have been incarcerated, and you are not?

Let me give you two perspectives of God interfering and not interfering. God's will was perfectly accomplished when Jesus went through trials on the night of his death. Someone looking in would have said it could not possibly be God's will for Jesus to suffer, but it was all part of God's perfect plan. There was a greater good being established, a larger purpose far beyond man's understanding. The pain and agony Christ endured was God's will as He implemented His plan for man's salvation and reconciliation to Himself. He knew the eventual outcome.

When Peter preached on the day of Pentecost, he told the crowd that what they had done to Jesus was exactly what God's will had predetermined would take place (Acts 2). To the unknowing, it appeared that God had not intervened, but He orchestrated the entire event. So God may seemingly not interfere, and there may be a seemingly terrible outcome that leads to an eventual greater good.

On the other hand, think of Mordecai in the book of Esther. Haman was trying to get Mordecai killed, but Mordecai was innocent of any offense. God intervened through Esther who went to the king and pleaded his case. The situation was flipped around, and Haman was killed instead.

If someone was guilty of a crime and God intervened, and the person received a pardon, that would be a demonstration of God's mercy. Remember, He does not always treat us as our sins deserve. So, plead for God's mercy if you are going to court. Thank Him that He is sovereign and ask for His will to be established in your life.

***A friend at work started a Powerball collection. Another friend
wants to know if it's okay to play.***

I had to check with the congregation to see what this was. Here is
my philosophy on gambling: If (1) all your debts are paid; (2) you
owe no man anything; (3) you have a certain entertainment
allotment in your budget that you use to go to movies or to play
games or for whatever type of entertainment you enjoy, then what
you do with your extra money is up to you. It's all part of your
disposable income.

Again, if you are not in debt to anyone, and you have a
certain amount of entertainment money that you think you want to
just throw away, then that's up to you. What you do with it is your
business. The money you put down on lottery tickets at the corner
liquor store or at the local gas station doesn't go to the schools, and
the odds are you are probably not going to win. You are basically
taking money and throwing it in the wind.

Is it wise? What do you think? Is it being a good steward
of what God has blessed you with? I could suggest more
constructive ways to invest your money, such as helping the poor
or supporting missionaries, supporting ministries at the church, etc.

If you are gambling, hoping against hope that you are
going to get rich, you need to stop. Maybe you are thinking to
yourself, "I'm going to get rich! Even if I spend money that I owe
somebody, I don't care. I'm going to go for this because, if I win, I

can pay off my debt." If this is the case, then you have some character issues that need to be addressed.

Some people think when they get "the big win" they will change their habits and suddenly become generous, or they will start tithing. If you are not tithing now, you won't tithe then.

Are people born emotional or do they become emotional?

Not long ago, when babies were born, doctors used to turn them upside down and whack them on the bottom. And what was the first thing those babies began doing? They began crying; they began displaying emotions.

God gave us emotions, and we are to manage them – just as we are to manage our appetites and our sex drives. We are to control our emotions; our emotions should not control us. This is often easier said than done. In the heat of any given moment, you may feel as if you have no power over your feelings and reactions. However, if you take the time to feel, acknowledge, breathe, and think, you will recognize that you do not have to give in to every emotion that comes your way. For instance, maybe you feel suddenly angry at someone. Take a moment to acknowledge the emotion: You feel angry. Don't act as if the feeling is not there. Owning it can help you respond appropriately. So feel it and acknowledge it. Take time to breathe and ask God for wisdom. Now you are ready to move forward.

We get so used to our emotions controlling us instead of the other way around. It doesn't have to be that way. It shouldn't be that way. In fact, walking in the Spirit is the best way to control emotions. One of the fruits of the Spirit is self control!

If God gave us emotions and feelings, why does He also tell us not to live by them?

God tells us that we are not to have a lifestyle that is controlled by our emotions. Paul told Timothy to keep his head in all situations (2 Timothy 4:5). What does that mean? It means, don't be foolish and lose your mind by way of your emotions. Keep your thinking apparatus, your intelligence and logic with you. Don't allow your emotions to surge either so low (depression) or so high (manic state) that you can't think straight and are unable to act reasonably.

Yes, God gave us emotions, but we are not to be driven or led by them. We are to manage them and control them and not allow them to manage or control us.

Even though the Bible says to honor your father and mother, what if it seems impossible to do so? How do you honor a mother who is hateful, hurtful, very abusive, and manipulative?

I don't know how old you are, but if you are eighteen or older, and she really is that way, you may need to remove yourself from that home. You have to set clear boundaries to let your mom know that you are not going to let her treat you in such a manner anymore.

If you can move out of her home, she cannot have such a negative impact on your life, and you can begin to rebuild yourself according to what God says about you and not according to the lies you have been hearing about yourself while under her roof. Then you can still honor her by forgiving her, praying for her, and still being nice to her. You can send her cards or gifts, even though you feel she doesn't deserve them.

You said it seems impossible to honor her; however, the Lord commands us to honor our parents, and He would not command us to do something that is impossible. You must begin to think of it in another way. Although she has not been a faithful example of what a mother should be, she gave you life.

You do not have to allow her to manipulate you. You do not have to participate with her in hateful, hurtful, or manipulative behavior. You can decide when and how you will spend time with her.

Now, if you are a teenager and you are unable to move out, then you need to come see one of the pastors and let us help you. But if you are of age, then it's time for you to go.

I believe I am walking in God's perfect will, but I am attacked constantly and viewed negatively. If the current position I am in is truly God's will, would I be so discouraged and attacked?

The attacks very well may be because you are walking in His perfect will. Keep up the good work and continue living your life according to what God says is right. Know that because you are walking in God's will, the enemy is going to attack you to try to discourage you. You do not want to give in to that discouragement. You want to be encouraged. I have some homework for you: Read 1 Peter. It says that if you are being persecuted, ridiculed, or abused for the name of Jesus, rejoice and glorify God. In other words, don't let the attacks discourage you. Take heart and be encouraged in the Lord.

Your faith is revealed in difficulty. You will learn whether you behave more like Christ or more like the world. If you feel you want to change jobs or whatever it may be, then it is okay to ask the Lord to open a door for you. In the meantime, keep praising Him and keep seeking Him. Keep loving your enemies and praying for them. There are lessons to be learned in all of this.

When you are doing right, the wrath of hell may be unleashed against you because the enemy of your soul does not want you living for Christ. So, of course, he will do whatever he can to destroy your joy and peace. Do not allow him to do so. Remember Colossians 3:15, which states, "Let the peace of Christ rule in your hearts, since as members of one body you were called to peace. And be thankful."

Also, I encourage you to take inventory of your behaviors and attitudes. Ask the Lord to show you areas in your life where you may need to improve to make the work situation more pleasant.

Are we not to fellowship or eat with a believer who is living in sin? (This is a two-part question. The first part is answered here, and the second part follows.)

Listen carefully to the wording – "believers" who are living in sin. If you know a friend or family member who absolutely calls himself a Christian but is living in blatant sin, you are to warn him, encourage him, try to talk him out of the sin, and do whatever you can to help him. As a last resort, you may have to tell him that you cannot hang out with him anymore because he is calling himself a believer but won't turn from his known, unashamed, disobedient sin. You let him know that you cannot walk with him until he repents.

It is Scripture, and you want to be careful (see 1 Corinthians 5). Again, this Scripture should be applied only after talking with this person and giving him or her time to repent.

This question goes on to ask, *"What if it's a family member? Do we still bring him to church even if he doesn't show desire or will or want to live differently?*

If someone calls himself a Christian, but does not show a desire or a will to live differently, I question that person's salvation. Many people call themselves Christians but demonstrate absolutely no change of lifestyle. A person may believe that because he attended church every Sunday since he was seven years old, it makes him a Christian. This is not so. Titus said that many people say Jesus is their Lord but, by their actions, they deny him (Titus 1:16). So, if there is a family member who is saying that he is saved but does not want to attend church or walk with God, well, one would have to wonder about the reality of that person's commitment to Christ.

What version of the Bible do you recommend for easy reading?

The *New International Version* is a good one to start with. It's written at a seventh to eighth grade reading level. I usually read from it for our sermons because it's written in a way that the average person can understand. The *New King James Version* is also written at a seventh to eighth grade reading level. For easier reading, you might consider The *New Living Translation.* The *New American Standard Version* is the most accurate Greek to English translation; but is slightly more challenging reading. It's written at about an eighth to eleventh grade reading level. (Of course, the grade levels are approximations.)

Choose one you like as long as it doesn't dis-empower the meaning of the text. Most translations are good. There are also a couple of new ones out, but I have not spent time studying them. A great one to read, just as an aside, is *The Message* by Eugene Peterson (written at about a fourth to fifth grade reading level). Peterson does a fabulous job with the text, but I would not recommend you use *The Message* as your main study Bible. If you really want *extra explan*ation, get an *Amplified Bible*; it contains expanded explanations of words and phrases, and the text is written at approximately a tenth grade reading level.

CHAPTER 3

The Church and Preaching

Does a seeker-friendly church dilute the power of God?

I cannot speak for all of them; that would be presumptuous and unfair. The term "seeker friendly" means a church is trying to reach un-churched people. To do that, and in an attempt to make "seekers" feel comfortable, a seeker-friendly church adjusts the Christian message to some degree. The music may be modified and the message diluted to make them both more acceptable to a non-Christian audience. If being seeker-sensitive is an effort to simply bring in crowds, but people are not hearing the Gospel, and lives are not being transformed, changed, and born again, then there is definitely a problem with that.

If a church that is seeker-friendly on Sundays uses its mid-week service to bring the full teaching of Christ, then that seems fairly appropriate. However, the majority of people attend church on Sundays and not during mid week. In this case, many people remain ignorant. Surely there are some seeker-friendly churches that do present the full Gospel message; however, there are some that do not.

I have gone to many churches and have not sensed the Spirit of God. I judge those churches. Am I wrong?

Yes. Be careful not to judge a church on one visit. You should sense the presence of God in a church – through the worship, teaching, prayers, etc. I wouldn't counsel someone to go to a particular church unless there was evidence of the following: solid and accurate Bible teaching, a sense of God's presence in worship, people who are loving and accepting, a safe and strong Sunday school, a good youth group, and a desire to see the lost saved.

These are some of the things one would look for in finding a church. You say you are "judging" other churches? "Judgment" in the sense of condemning would not be the right approach, but once you have been in a loving, Spirit-filled church where the Word is rightly taught, it would be difficult to attend one that is lacking in these attributes.

I am new to this church. On the wall, it says, "Tribe of Judah." What does that mean?

Tribe of Judah is the name of our worship team. Judah was one of the twelve tribes of Israel. The nation of Israel began with a man named Abraham. When Abraham was an elderly man, God promised him a son. Abraham was about one hundred years old, and his wife, Sara, was ninety when their son was born. They named the child Isaac. Isaac grew to manhood and had twin boys, Jacob and Esau.

Jacob's name was later changed to Israel. He grew to manhood and had twelve sons. His fourth son's name was Judah. His mother named him Judah because she said, "This time I will praise the Lord" (Genesis 29:35). The name Judah means *praise*.

Each of Israel's sons established his own tribe. If you follow the line of Judah, you will find that Kind David came from his line. The Messiah was to be the son of David, meaning He would come from David's (hence Judah's) line of ancestry. Jesus came from the tribe of Judah. He is even called the *Lion of the tribe of Judah*.

When we first moved here, we had a worship band and one day during prayer, I came up with the name Tribe of Judah, meaning "a band of praise."

A lady spoke in tongues last Sunday and then she gave the interpretation. Then a man spoke. Was that a double interpretation of what was spoken in tongues?

No. A sister gave us a message in tongues and gave the interpretation. A brother then stood up and read Psalm 37. He read it as an encouragement, an exhortation, and a comfort. Psalm 37:4 says, "Take delight in the Lord, and He will grant you the desires of your heart." So it was not a continuation of the message in tongues. It was an encouragement for the body.

What is your opinion of Benny Hinn?

Benny Hinn is a brother in the Lord. I think some of his tactics are suspect. For some reason, instead of being an evangelist and a faith healer, he decided to be a theologian. As a result, he got himself out on a few theological tangents that he should have never tried to tackle and made himself look a bit silly. He has since recanted and is just trying to do the work of God as an evangelist. Regarding the miracles, some say they are genuine, others say they are not. I've also heard reports that many of the so-called miracles cannot be medically substantiated. I am somewhat skeptical based on things I've heard and read; however, his autobiography is well worth the read. If you are going to go see him, I would advise you to chew the meat and throw out the bones. You always want to listen to a man's doctrine. That is what is important. What is the doctrine, and does it line up with Scripture?

What is the procedure to become a member of this church? I truly desire to be a member of this family.

We do have an awesome group of people here. First off, know that if you are saved, you are part of the body of Christ. You already belong. To become a member of our local church body, we ask that you attend our new member's class. It's an opportunity for you to be introduced to the pastors and the staff, and we'll familiarize you with our various ministries. If you are already saved, you can fill out the membership card now and attend the class when it is next offered. (Classes occur every quarter.) If you want to become a member, we want to know you, and we want you to know us. Attending the class is important.

Can you speak on preachers who were preaching that the world would end in 2012 and that Jesus would come on a certain day?

You ask me to comment on the preachers who were preaching that nonsense? Let the nullification of the prophecy speak for itself. Do not follow nonsense.

I feel sorry and disappointed that fellow preachers would allow themselves that kind of mistake in leading their congregations. The Bible has been and must always be our guide. There have been so many "false dates" through the years which only serve to prove the Bible is right. The Bible teaches that no man knows the day or the hour... (Matthew 24:36).

The Mayan calendar predicted that the world would end in 2012. However, we have something that trumps the Mayan calendar! Hopefully, you did not sell your house or put off paying your bills in the hope that the end was at hand. What would be the point of selling your house anyway? If the world was truly going to end in 2012, and let's say you knew that, what good would it have done to have more money in the bank? It doesn't make sense. The end means the end. Everything would be over.

Keep working, keep serving God, and keep on trusting Him to take care of you. Love your family, share your faith, encourage others to live for the Lord, and set a good example. Be a godly man or woman when others are watching and especially when they are not. Keep on living.

When is the last time there has been a great spiritual revival in the Bay Area – a week of loving God, fasting, prayer, and pure worship?

A week of loving God does not define a revival. I don't know of any particular revival, but God continues to save people through Gospel preaching churches in this area. I know that many churches like ours feel like we have been in a perpetual revival. Has the church body across the Bay Area really come together and consecrated itself and set itself apart? No.

What if we called a week of fasting and prayer? I believe many in our congregation would join in, and that could start a revival. Revival means that the church gets revived and, from the overflow of that, the lost start coming.

If you want to read some good historical books on Christianity, read about some of the great revivals such as the Great Awakenings in America, Wales, and England when preachers were sold out to God, and hundreds of thousands of people were getting saved.

In the late 1700's, there was a major revival occurring along the East Coast. According to some accounts, as clipper ships off the coast of New England were sailing near land, the men on board began falling down (for no apparent reason) and crying out to God, begging Him to save them.

There was a time in Wales when a preacher arrived and began to preach to the working men. The coal miners were getting saved so quickly that they had to retrain the work mules. The mules were only used to responding to swear words and foul language and had to be retrained to respond to their masters' new lives and clean language.

Revival is a divine move of the Holy Spirit as pastors and preachers set themselves apart to God, and as the Body of Christ responds in repentance, faith, and prayers for the lost.

I love Sunday worship and traditionally have always worshiped on Sundays. However, what is the history of the change to the Sabbath on Sunday rather than the Old Testament and New Testament Sabbath day on Saturday?

The church went from worshiping on a Saturday, which God commanded the Jews to do, to worshiping on a Sunday because it was a celebration of the resurrection of our Lord. The Apostle Paul wrote, "One person considers one day more sacred than another; another considers every day alike. Each of them should be fully convinced in their own mind" (Romans 14:5). Seventh Day Adventists and Jewish people believe Saturday is the day to worship. To them we say, *Do as you like, but do not require that we worship on the same day.*

Scripture has given us freedom to worship on this day or that day or any day. We can worship every day. In fact, our very lives are to be worship unto the Lord. We simply come together corporately in Jesus' name on Sundays to celebrate the resurrection of Christ.

Is the Sabbath day on Saturday or Sunday?

Saturday was the original Sabbath. The first day of the week is Sunday; the last day would be Saturday. Under the new covenant, people began to celebrate the Sabbath, the day of rest, on Sunday. For Christians, the Sabbath became Sunday because Jesus rose on that day. It was a day of celebration of Christ's resurrection. Remember, the Sabbath was made for man, not man for the Sabbath. God gave us a day to rest our body.

How many of you actually take that commandment seriously? What if you take one day a week to rest your body? You might become a more productive, all-around nicer person.

What is your belief regarding extraterrestrials and aliens? They scare me to death. Please tell me they are not real.

Well, I could just say, "Okay, they are not real." I could also tell you that I have talked to and listened to many great Bible scholars who do believe that there is life in the universe besides ours. We know there are angels, and we know there are spirits. Elijah was taken up in a whirlwind. The person writing that story in 2 Kings said it looked like a chariot of fire and horses of fire. He used words that were familiar to him. What was it he saw? Would we describe it as a spaceship today? What words would we use?

John, who wrote the Book of Revelation, saw things that are yet to happen, but he didn't know how to put what he saw in the common vernacular because he didn't have a point of reference to be able to describe it all. Two thousand years ago, how would he describe an airplane? How would he describe a missile? What terms would he use?

You don't have to worry about extraterrestrials. You are blood bought, blood washed, and covered by Jesus Christ. You are fine. Christ's love is perfect. Why are you afraid? Do not fear the unknown. Do you not trust the love of Christ? Trust Him.

CHAPTER 4

Death and Dying

Is a person crazy to be comfortable when it's time to die if he or she is saved in Jesus Christ?

I think "comfortable" is the only way to go. At the end of life, a believer can have the confidence to say, "Lord, I'm ready. I've had enough of this place." Those who remain behind sometimes need help releasing their loved ones. We must be willing to let our loved ones go.

I recently received a call regarding a ninety year old mother who was slowly dying. The family said, "We don't want to pull the plug. We love her." The doctors said that the woman was suffering greatly. What was the family holding on to? The woman had lived a full life, and now her physical body was shutting down.

Why were they keeping her alive? Were they keeping her alive for her own sake or for themselves?

We have to be ready to let go. The death rate is one per person. Everyone is going to die. We are going to die one of five ways: war, murder, accident, disease, or old age. The good news for us, as believers, is that we have hope. An amazing future awaits us!

If we are with God or present with the Lord as soon as we die, when the Rapture occurs, will we go back in our bodies to be judged? How do we go to Heaven before the judgment day?

Paul wrote, "We are confident, I say, and would prefer to be away from the body and at home with the Lord" (2 Corinthians 5:8). Paul also wrote, "I desire to depart and be with Christ, which is better by far; but it is more necessary for you that I remain in the body" (Philippians 1:23-24).

We believe that when we die, our spirit or soul goes to be with the Lord, and our body is buried (or cremated) and returns to dust (or ashes). On the Day of the Lord, we will be raised with a new body. Our spirit will meet our new body in the air, and we will ever be with the Lord. Believers who are still alive at that time will meet the Lord in the air. Their bodies will be transformed into heavenly bodies. See 1 Thessalonians 4:13-17 and Philippians 3:20-21.

There are different views in Christian thinking as to when this will happen, whether it will be pre-tribulation, mid-tribulation, or post-tribulation. Whichever position you hold, we all understand and agree that each of us will receive a new, glorified body for all eternity.

Is cremation allowed?

Yes, it is. It's also usually much less expensive than burial. The body goes to dust no matter what you do with it. Somebody asked whether it's harder for the Lord to put it back together if it's cremated. Well, perhaps so, but He can do it, so it's okay. Isn't it interesting that we would believe that the God who created the universe and who created man from the dust of the ground would be unable to do something because it was "hard"? He is God. Buried or cremated, He will know exactly where your body is.

What happens to Christians when they die? Do they go to Abraham's bosom, or do they just fall asleep and go straight to heaven or what?

There are two places in the New Testament where the Apostle Paul refers to the fact that to die is to enter the Lord's presence.

In Philippians 1, Paul wrote that to die is to go and be with Christ, and this is better by far than remaining here on earth.

Paul was in a dilemma. He was under house arrest, and he didn't know if his life was going to end or not. At the same time, he felt he had a certain say-so in the matter. In essence, Paul concluded, "I am going to remain with you for a while because you need me, so I am not going to die right now. If I did die now, I would be with the Lord."

In 2 Corinthians 5:8, Paul wrote that to be absent from the body is to be present with the Lord.

These two Scriptures alone seem to annihilate any teaching regarding purgation. Purgation is time in purgatory, the place some people believe you go if you are not quite good enough to go to heaven and not quite bad enough to go to hell. According to Roman Catholic doctrine, you may be genuinely saved, but because you are not purged of all your sins, you cannot yet enter into heaven. Catholicism bases this belief on Matthew 5:8 which says, "Blessed are the pure in heart for they shall see God," and teaches that because you were not pure when you died, because there were sins on you when you died, you need to go through a time of purging to purify yourself before you are allowed entrance into paradise. Purgatory is like a temporary holding cell.

In the front of the Catholic Douay Bible, it says that for every fifteen minutes you read your Bible, you get three hundred days out of purgatory. This is what it says; I am not making this up. In earlier times, one of the ways the Catholic Church offered souls release from purgatory was by selling indulgences. If you paid a certain amount of money, you could get a relative or loved one released from purgatory sooner than he or she would normally be released.

None of this is biblical; it's not Scripture. Practices like these spurred the Protestant Reformation. Protestants are people who protested. They protested against the organization of the Roman Catholic Church promoting extra-biblical teachings such as purgatory, the Doctrine of Mary, the veneration of saints, the Immaculate Conception, and so on.

So, for Paul, to die would be gain. It would be advancement. To be absent from the body is to immediately be present with the Lord.

Why is the loss of someone so hard even when you are a believer?

We grieve when saved, loved ones die – we just do not to grieve like the rest of the world. Jesus wept when He visited the tomb of His friend Lazarus who had died (John 11:35). He saw the deep sorrow and pain death caused. Grief and sadness are human emotions. When we lose people we love, we hurt.

Why does it hurt when they die? They have touched our lives, and they will be missed. They were a part of who we are. We are not going to get to kiss their faces or talk to them any more in this life. It hurts because we are human beings; we feel pain, and loss, and heartache. *Not grieving as the world does* is a reminder for us as believers. We know that we will see them again one day because we have the promise of eternal life. That's the good part that makes grieving different for us. We have hope in a future beyond this short life here on earth.

It is very human and God-like to grieve. It's okay to feel the pain of separation. Remember, life is short. We won't be around forever.

Our time here on earth is too short to stay angry at folks. Too often, we wait until we lose someone we love and then wish we had reached out to the person more. Tell folks you love them as often as you can and practice regular, small acts of kindness toward people. Let people know they matter and that you care.

When my time is finished here on earth, and I do make it through the pearly gates, will I then become pure and sinless like my Lord?

Yes, you will, because the Bible says we can look forward to a new heaven and a new earth, "...where righteousness dwells" (2 Peter 3:13). Nothing foul, evil, or sinful shall be there.

How does one find joy after losing a parent?

You're probably not going to have joy after losing a parent, not for a while. The joy you will have is the inner peace of knowing your mom or dad is with Jesus.

Losing a parent is a grievous thing. As Christians, however, we don't mourn like the world does. The world has no hope after a loved one dies. Many people believe that our bodies are simply energy and atoms. They believe that death is the ultimate end; whereas, we know that death is really the beginning of eternal life.

My dad has been gone for twenty years, and I still cry about it sometimes. My mom has been gone five years, and I still miss her. I have very wonderful memories of both of them. The joy comes in knowing they were good parents, and they loved me. They nurtured and taught me as best they could. They passed on their history to me and gave me a legacy to pass on to my children.

As you remember your mom or dad, you can thank God for the opportunity you had to share life with each of them. You had a loving relationship, and that's something to smile about. You can also rejoice that you were brought up in a good home. You can still honor your deceased parents by speaking well of them and serving God as you know you should.

The pain will lessen with time. Grief is a process. Give yourself time.

What does it mean when dead loved ones come to you with joy and happiness?

I don't know who the people are that came to you. The enemy does deceive, and he is an imitator. Paul said the devil can masquerade himself as an angel of light, but he is really an angel of darkness. I would like to know more of the experiences you've had with these so-called spirits of people who have gone on and are coming back to talk to you. More than likely, the enemy is trying to confuse your mind. Scripture does not confirm that departed people communicate with those of us who are still alive.

My grandpa died without accepting Christ as his Savior. Is there anything I can do to help him at all?

This is a very tough question, and my answer is going to be very difficult for you to hear. First, do you really know that he was not saved? We often don't really know what people are thinking in their final moments. We won't know until we get to heaven whether someone had a change of heart as he or she neared that final breath. God is an amazing God, and he can reach people even on their death beds. So, in that sense, we really just don't know.

The Bible says it is appointed unto man once to die, and then comes the judgment (Hebrews 9:27). Protestant Christian orthodox theology informs us regarding this. When people have taken their last breath, if they have not accepted Jesus Christ as their Savior, there is nothing we can do. We do not pray for the dead.

My hope is that someone shared the Gospel with your grandfather during his lifetime. I hope that he always had it in the back of his mind but maybe was too stubborn to give in and maybe, in his last few moments, cried out to God before he died.

We don't know, so this is the hope we have at this time.

It is a reminder to us all to share our faith.

Do kids who die and go to heaven grow up?

I believe they take on an eternal body. I believe they come to a place of maturity that does not age.   Before the age of accountability, whatever that may be, the Bible seems to say that they do go to heaven.

What does it mean that the dead in Christ will rise?

When Jesus returns, all Christians who have died will have their earthly bodies miraculously transformed into heavenly eternal bodies, just like the resurrected body of the Lord himself. Paul says it will happen in a flash, in the twinkling of an eye, at the last trumpet blast (1 Corinthians 15:52). "For the Lord himself will come down from heaven, with a loud command, with the voice of the archangel and with the trumpet call of God, and the dead in Christ will rise first. After that, we who are still alive and are left will be caught up together with them in the clouds to meet the Lord in the air. And so we will be with the Lord forever" (1 Thessalonians 4:16-17).

No matter what has happened to our former bodies, whether we have been cremated, eaten by animals, lost at sea, or buried – by a miracle of God, our spirits, which went directly to the Lord at death, will be united with our new bodies, and forever we shall be with the Lord. This is why we do not grieve like the world grieves when we lose a loved one. We will not only see them again, but we will be with them again.

If you die in your sins, can you still enter the kingdom? What if death occurs unexpectedly during backsliding or struggling in sin?

First of all, let's clearly define what we mean by dying in your sins. When Jesus said to the Pharisees, "If you do not believe I am who I say I am, you will die in your sins"(John 8:24), he was talking about unbelievers who did not accept him as Savior and Messiah.

Those who reject Christ are still under the curse of sin which leads to eternal separation from God. This is totally different from someone who has given his or her life to Christ, is born again, and has the Spirit of God living in within.

As believers, we all still sin from time to time (okay, daily). We are to confess our sins (daily) to stay in close communion with God. If a Christian is still weak in an area, or has a hard time in a particular area of life and suddenly dies without having confessed that sin, the person is still saved and is still a child of God. You don't lose your Salvation every time you blow it or do something foolish.

However, if a person says he or she is saved but gives little or no evidence of a changed life and simply continues to live a life of habitual, blatant sin, we could question whether that individual ever truly really surrendered his or her life to Christ as Lord. Take a look at 1 Corinthians 5 and 1 John 2.

What about when animals die? Do animals have souls?

We know that there are horses in heaven because Jesus is coming back on a white horse. I don't see in Scripture where it says an animal has a spirit like a human does. They are created creatures for the earth.

Where does it say in the Bible that dogs do not go to heaven?

Where in the Bible does it say that they do? It doesn't say they do or they don't. Scripture says that when God created man, He breathed into him the breath of life, and man became a living being – made in the image of God, an eternal being. It doesn't say that about the animals. But if you believe that your Chihuahua, Stanley, or your hound, Tucker, will greet you in Heaven... well, Okay!

CHAPTER 5

Does God Care About Me?

How do you know whether God has forsaken you?

God has not forsaken you. Why would you think that He has? There is an old saying which I don't like, but it fits: *If God seems far away, who moved?*

God will not forsake you. How do I know that? Scripture tells us so. He says in His Word, "I will never leave you or forsake you" (Hebrews 13:5). Jesus said, "And surely I am with you always, to the very end of the age" (Matthew 28:20).

Jesus said, "All that the Father gives Me will come to Me, and the one who comes to Me I will by no means cast out" (John 6:37). That is how it is stated in the *New King James Version.* In the *NIV* it says, "All those the Father gives me will come to me, and whoever comes to me I will never drive away." So, you see, God has not forsaken you. He has not cast you to the side or kicked you to the curb. He has not forgotten you, your tears, or your struggles. You are not alone in this world.

You feel alone, and you feel that God has left you. Again, please hear me, God has *not* left you. Lift up your hands to God right now, right in this moment. Tell Him you feel alone. Pour out your heart to Him. It's okay to be honest with God. Let Him know your doubts and fears. Tell Him you need Him. He will meet with you and make Himself known to you. His Word promises that if we belong to Him, He is always with us.

You must get around some people who can encourage you. Do you have friends who love the Lord? We are not meant to walk this life alone. The world is full of heartache and difficulty. You need friends and people in your life who love Jesus, people who will come along side you during the dry and barbed seasons that beset us all at some time or another, people who will speak life into you.

Jesus said, "In this world you will have trouble. But take heart! I have overcome the world" (John 16:33). There is emphasis and strength in that command. Take heart! Be encouraged! It was time for Jesus to suffer and die. He knew his disciples would scatter. He knew they would feel disillusioned and abandoned. They would experience great disappointment and confusion. But he encouraged them and offered them his peace. Do not give up! Do not give in to the lies of the enemy! It's like he was telling his disciples, "Trust God! Just trust me! Hold onto me. This life will not be easy. There will be trials. At times you will feel all alone, but you must trust me. I have overcome this world, and you will too. But you must trust me."

Life is difficult, but the God of the universe knows your name, and He has not forsaken or forgotten you. You must reach out to Him. He has a plan and a purpose for your life. James 4:8 says, "Come near to God and He will come near to you."

Pastor, how come I feel like God has forsaken me?

God has not forsaken you. The devil is lying to you, speaking words and drawing pictures in your mind that are not true. Listen, you have to do what every other Christian has to do. You must actively pull down every thought that goes against what the Word says about God's love for you. You must not give in to the lies of the enemy. The Lord said, "Never will I leave you; never will I forsake you" (Hebrews 13:5). In the Greek that wording is emphatic; it's redundant. It's like saying *I will never, never, ever, ever, never, ever leave you.* How about that? He wants us to grasp the concept. He wants us to understand this truth.

There is so much that comes against us in life. Sometimes it feels as though life itself is against us. When you feel like God has forsaken you, what do you do? How do you live? Maybe you begin to live like there is no tomorrow, or you act as if your actions have no consequences. Maybe you behave foolishly and recklessly because you feel alone. Maybe you lash out at others and are cruel and unkind because you feel so empty inside. Maybe you give up and just don't care about anything anymore, or you do things that are harmful to yourself. How's that working for you?

Listen, God is with you. If you feel abandoned and alone, tell the Lord how and what you feel. Ask for His help. Whisper a prayer, "Help me, Lord Jesus." Let it be the true cry of your heart. Repeat it in moments when you feel alone and helpless. The Lord hears and recognizes the cries of His children.

Are you reading your Bible? Jesus says, "If you love me, keep my commands. And I will ask the Father, and He will give you another advocate to help you and to be with you forever – the Spirit of truth..." (John 14:15-17). This is the Holy Spirit. If you ask, the Lord will guide you as you read the Word. When you open your Bible and read, ask the Holy Spirit to make the words real for you.

Begin to recite Scripture verses. Learn and memorize them. The Holy Spirit will show you the truth of Scripture that assures us that we are never, ever alone. God will never leave you. He will never forsake you, and you will come to know and walk in this truth once you begin to learn who your Father God really is.

Paul encourages us with these words: "Who shall separate us from the love of Christ? Shall trouble or hardship or persecution or famine or nakedness or danger or sword? ...No, in all these things we are more than conquerors though him who loved us. For I am convinced that neither death nor life, neither angels nor demons, neither the present nor the future, nor any powers, neither height nor depth, nor anything else in all creation, will be able to separate us from the love of God that is in Christ Jesus our Lord" (Romans 8:35-39).

Begin to live trusting that God has not forsaken you. How much trust in God do you need to begin making changes in your life? How much faith is necessary? Just a tiny little bit. A baby step of faith, a little trust is all you need.

What would you do differently if you knew that God was always present, always with you, always caring? Think about these questions for a moment – How would you live and behave if you absolutely knew God was in your corner? Would you reach out to others more? Maybe you'd be a little kinder, a little more patient? Would you have more joy? If you knew God was for you, would you practice gratitude? Would you be thankful for the things you take for granted each day? Take one of these areas and begin practicing now. Start trusting God and see how your life changes.

You also need godly friendships. I wonder if you are isolating yourself. You must get around others of the same sex who love the Lord. Spend time together talking and laughing and enjoying life. Please consider getting connected through a ministry, a home group, or a Bible study. It will make a difference for you. You need a place to share life with others. I hope to hear from you again to know how you are doing.

I am trying to trust Jesus. But I feel like no matter how much I go to church and pray, I still feel lost and confused. What else can I do so I don't feel sad or confused all the time?

It sounds like you have not been saved for a long time. Did you have bouts of depression before you got saved? Is the depression organic or situational? If it is organic (meaning you have always struggled throughout your life), then when you get saved, it doesn't mean depression is automatically reversed. You will need to seek professional care and, if necessary, be given medication to help you function normally.

If it is a situational or a "thought-processed" depression (meaning something happened to you, or there continues to be something in your thought patterns that keeps you stuck in sadness), then you haven't yet learned to combat it.

Our minds are filled with all types of negative thinking. Our thoughts get crowded with life's circumstances and the craziness of just living. We grow stronger, healthier and more content by learning the Word of God and by worshiping and praising Him. Again, if the sadness is not organic, you can begin to train your mind to center itself on the Lord. For instance, when you come into a worship service, really allow yourself to focus on the greatness and goodness of God. Give yourself permission to enter His presence. The Bible says God will give you a garment of praise for the spirit of heaviness (Isaiah 61:3). Begin to put on that garment – clothe yourself with praise of the Lord Jesus Christ.

If you struggle beyond that, please make an appointment so that you can talk with us or with your pastor. Realize that you also might need to see a doctor. If medication is necessary, there's nothing wrong with that.

I have a friend who is dealing with anxiety. She is a new Christian. She reads the Word, prays, and worships, but the attacks still come. What should she do?

It sounds like the patterns of her thinking will need to be renewed or changed. Romans 12:2 urges us to be transformed by the renewing of our minds. How do we do this? We read God's Word;

we learn it and memorize it. When we feel anxious, we learn to rely on what the Word says. We do not allow fear to control our lives. Fear, if allowed, has the power to cripple and dominate us. We must not let it. Philippians 4 tells us that the peace of God is available to us, and this peace will guard our hearts and minds in Christ Jesus.

Talking with a counselor or pastor is vitally important. Sometimes we try to fix ourselves. Conversation with someone trained to help us with these kinds of issues can dramatically change our lives. God does not want us living in fear and worry. He promises us peace. Please have your friend make an appointment to speak with a pastor. We need to find out if the source of the anxiety is organic, situational, or just a pattern of her thinking. This will determine how the problem can be addressed. There can be issues from early childhood or situations even more recent which are affecting her and causing this anxiety.

Is it okay to take psych medication? Does God like a person who is on that kind of medication?

Are you asking if you would be in sin for taking medication? Has your medication been doctor prescribed and deemed necessary? Are you taking it because you truly need it, not because it gives you a high or because you are addicted to it? If your reasons for taking medication are legitimate, do you feel God would object to it? If you are really in mental or physical pain, then you might need medication. If your brain has a chemical imbalance, and medication will help even out your mental condition, then do what you need to do. There is no shame in that.

If medication is doctor prescribed because the doctor doesn't have time to see you, remember that he or she is only one doctor with one opinion, and you might want to get a second opinion to make sure the first one is what is best for you.

You should also be aware that the pharmaceutical industry is big business. In many ways, modern medicine has become a form of legalized drug dealing. Think about it. If you walk into many doctors' offices with an issue of almost any kind, you are going to be advised to take some type of medication. Someone is making money from it. You have a responsibility to be educated. It's okay to get a second and even a third opinion.

Let me take this a little further and address those who are taking medication for the wrong reasons. God is very concerned with the motivation of your heart. Are you hooked on legal meds? By taking medication, are you trying to make an excuse for doing something you know is wrong? If so, know that you are getting away with something now, but in the long run you are hurting yourself. You get loaded on it, and your body gets used to it because it's an addiction. Then you can't get off of it. You make excuses by saying things like "my back is sore" or "I have these headaches," and you keep popping pills when you know you have an addiction problem. Think of the damage you are doing to your body. Over time, any kind of narcotic will devastate your liver. Not only are you destroying yourself, but your loved ones are suffering. You may not be able to see it because you are so focused on your addiction. Addiction creates a very selfish and self-focused life. You need to get help.

I also suggest you meet with our prayer team. We have had many healings when people come forward in faith for prayer.

Getting back to the original question, you ask whether God likes a person who is on medication. My friend, God wants the best for you. Christ came, lived, died, and rose again for us all. Your being on medication has nothing to do with your value in His eyes. He looks at you, and He sees the value of the person you are – the person He created. He sees the potential you cannot see, and He calls you beloved. I invite you to join a *Celebrate Recovery* group and begin learning just how much your Father God loves you, even you. He loves you unconditionally!

CHAPTER 6

Suicide

Pastor, I do not understand. If someone killed himself, but he believed in God, why would he go to hell?

My friend, your question poses two thoughts. First, someone killed himself and, second, he believed in God. Allow me to answer the "believed in God" part first. Just believing in God is not enough. Even the devil believes in God. If anyone dies, no matter how, and has rejected Jesus as Lord, that person is headed for hell.

If you meant that the person was a Christian and committed suicide, that is different. I've said before that suicide is not the unpardonable sin. If the person was genuinely saved, committing suicide doesn't mean exclusion from heaven. Any Christian at any time may find himself or herself in a place of hopelessness and despair. It is an extremely grievous situation when a believer in Jesus Christ decides to take his or her own life. The person has given up on the hope the Lord offers and has succumbed to the lies of the devil. Very tragic.

Satan deceives the mind and convinces it that there is no way out of a difficult situation. The enemy lies and says, "You might as well go ahead and kill yourself." Satan is the enemy of your soul. Do you understand that? He does not want you to live. Satan's desire is to rob you of every possibility of a future by persuading you to take your life. He gets you to focus on the moment. He magnifies emotions of isolation, misunderstanding, confusion, loneliness, shame, regret, and despair.

It is all a tremendous lie. Suicide is not the answer.

The real truth is that you have a God who loves you. He knows what you are going through, and He wants you to live. God has a plan and a purpose for your life. Satan would love to thwart that plan. If you choose life and begin to walk with God, your life will eventually turn around.

Think about teenagers. Why do so many young people kill themselves when they are being bullied? For teenagers, peer pressure is often everything. It controls them and dominates their minds. When they feel like they are pushed out, not accepted, or made fun of, they can begin to feel very isolated and alone, and feelings of despair prevail. They lack self-esteem and a sense of self worth because they deeply lack God-awareness. They feel that there is no way out and that there is no one to protect them. They believe no one cares. Satan intensifies the mental torture and ups the ante. He convinces the mind that it's best to give up and that death would be a sweet release. The feelings become horribly overwhelming, and young people begin to feel that suicide is the only way out.

Satan is the god of hopelessness. God is a God of hope.

If you are in any way feeling that you want to end your life, you must tell somebody. You are not meant to carry these feelings alone. You must get help. No one was brought into this world to snuff out his or her own life. You are too precious and too valuable for that. Maybe you don't feel valuable right now. Maybe you feel like there is no motivation for you to live. But God gave you life – so there is a purpose for your being on this earth. Don't fool yourself into thinking there is no reason to live. You have so much to live for; you just don't know it yet. Part of the journey of life is finding out – but you have to give yourself time. Right now, in the thick of things, everything seems hopeless because you cannot see a future. The feelings of the moment are what they are; they are feelings, and they will not last forever. Give yourself the time to have hindsight – to one day look back on what was a very difficult season in your life, but you made it through.

We want to help heal your heart. God has not abandoned you. Call us and let's sit down and talk together. We can match you up with some friends who can walk through this difficult season of life with you.

Suicide is never, ever the answer.

I have heard that if you commit suicide that it is one of the biggest sins. Is this true? Someone I loved very much committed suicide. When my time is up, and I make it to heaven, will I see this person?

Well, if you don't see him in heaven, it won't be because he committed suicide. Suicide is not the unpardonable sin.

The unfortunate reality is that sometimes folks give up on life. Suicide is a way of saying there is no more hope, all hope is forever lost. Listen, as long as we live and breathe, there is always hope. Who is the one who steals our hope? Satan. He is the one who whispers, "It's never going to change. It's always going to be hard. It's always going to be just like it is. There is no out." A Christian can get himself in such a despondent place that he believes these lies and takes his own life.

Is it the biggest sin? Well, murder is a horrible sin. Adultery also destroys lives. Gossip ruins reputations. Molesting children damages them for the rest of their lives. Is suicide the unpardonable sin? I don't believe so.

We find no scriptural support which says that if a person is genuinely saved and commits suicide, he will go to hell. If you are saved, and the person in question was saved, I believe you will see him again.

Now, having said that, we must remember that suicide is never the answer to our problems – never, ever, ever. In the moment, it may feel like it is the only option, but there are other options. Reaching out and getting help (even if it means facing the consequences) is always the better option.

Suicide is a very selfish sin because the person who commits suicide leaves people behind who end up desperately hurt. Friends and loved ones suffer in heartache and grief as they try to pick up the pieces. They are left wondering why and trying to figure out what went wrong in the person's life that drove him to such a desperate action. Is this the kind of legacy we want to leave behind?

Choosing life is the best option. It takes courage to go on living and, if we ask, God will give us the strength to live through one day at a time.

If you have been considering suicide, PLEASE reach out! For immediate assistance, please call the National Suicide Prevention Lifeline at 1-800-273-TALK (8255).

CHAPTER 7

What About Alcohol, Weed, Jewelry, and Tattoos?

The Bible says that it is a sin to get drunk, but what if you're only tipsy? What if you have a high tolerance level?

You sound like you may be trying to figure out a way to sin and get away with it. Let's be honest. If you drink a glass of wine or have a drink, at some point, whether half-way or third-way through that glass, you are going to get tipsy.

You have to deal with yourself and the true motivations of your own heart on this issue. It's a matter of your truthfulness with the Lord. Where are you when you drink? Do you have to have that drink? Can you still think straight, walk straight, and talk straight? Can you not have that drink and still have a good time? Can you enjoy your dinner and relax without a glass of wine? Are you trying to prove that it's okay for you to drink? Could you stop? These are questions you have to ask yourself, and you have to honestly look at your drinking habits. Like I said, it really is a question of your own integrity before God. Drinking is not forbidden in Scripture, but drunkenness always is. Read Romans 14.

I was asked by my teenage son if marijuana was a tree or a plant. I told him that I believe it's a weed – pardon the pun. I said it's a weed planted in your garden to rob you of blessings. He replied that in the book of Genesis God said to use all the plants on the earth. Now I am confused. Did I lie to my son? He is not a young teenager or a stupid one. I think he asked to check out my response to see how far the conversation could go.

Second Peter, Chapter 3, says that there are some things hard to understand, which ignorant and unstable people twist, as they do other Scriptures, to their own destruction. Your son's statement is a classic example of distorting Scripture. Mom/Dad, you gave up too quickly. You were frozen by a question; you didn't have a quick enough answer, and so you got stuck. In the future, just calm down and wait for the wisdom to answer. Give yourself about twenty seconds or so and just breathe. In those few moments, ask God for wisdom.

Think about it. If God meant for us to eat all the plants, then ask your son if he would like to go out and eat the poison oak in the regional park. Would you ask him to eat some poisonous mushrooms or poison ivy? Of course you would not. Obviously, when God said, "I give you every seed-bearing plant on the face of the whole earth and every tree that has fruit with seed in it. They will be yours for food," He meant all the edible green plants (Genesis 1:29). Also, remember, this was before the fall of man. There was nothing that would have harmed mankind or have a negative effect on one's health.

Marijuana is a drug that alters your sense of being, and God doesn't want you controlled or mastered by anything except the Holy Spirit.

What is the church's stance on medical marijuana?

Medical marijuana is no different from medical cocaine, morphine, etc. It's a drug. Are you asking whether you should smoke medical marijuana? Well, do you have a true medical condition that could be helped by it? What is your purpose, and what is the motive? Are you trying to slip under the radar because you want to go to your doctor and claim you have some condition, so he can prescribe medical marijuana for you to go get high? If so, do you really think you are passing under the radar of God? Remember, God looks beyond what you are doing. He looks to your motive. If you don't truly need it, leave it alone. Medicines are made to help people. The side effects of many drugs can be worse than the condition. Too many people become addicted to prescription meds, and medical marijuana could be addictive as well.

What is your position on tattoos and Christians? Is it okay for Christians to get tattoos or not?

Even within our congregation there may be much disagreement on this issue. If you get a tattoo of a skull and a pitchfork, that could be a problem. I have a tattoo on my arm. It's a picture of a cross with a dove landing on it, and there is blood dripping from the cross. It is my way of saying I am a Christian, and nothing is going to change that.

The New Testament is completely silent about the issue; however, in the Old Testament, the Jews were instructed not to put any tattoos on their bodies (Leviticus 19:28). The purpose of the restriction was to set the Jews apart from all the other nations, especially since what most people from other nations put on their bodies was ungodly.

Please remember, a tattoo is on for the rest of your life. Think about it before you go putting something on yourself that you might later regret.

My fiancé and I work in fields where we cannot wear our rings, so we are planning on getting the rings tattooed on us with our names in them. Is it a sin to get those done?

Getting your rings tattooed is not a sin, but maybe there is another way. Can you wear the ring on a chain around your neck? Can you agree on something else as a statement in place of a wedding ring? If you decide to go ahead with the tattoo rings, I would advise that you don't get them until after you are married. Things can change right up until the actual vows are spoken.

Should Christian men wear earrings?

I think you are asking if it is okay for a Christian man to wear an earring. It's jewelry. It's amoral: neither good nor bad. What statement are you trying to make by wearing an earring? Nowadays, we see men wearing two earrings. In the Old

Testament, Absalom had earrings and nose rings and belly button rings and so on. We didn't invent this stuff.

What are you trying to prove with it? If you are doing it to look weird or ridiculous – why? If you are doing it to establish your personality or to fit in – why do you feel you have to go to such lengths? That's something you have to deal with within yourself. Are you doing it as a rebellious act? I've seen those earrings that stretch out and blow up the bottom part of the ear. I just say, "Go on with your bad self."

There is nothing intrinsically evil or sinful with jewelry. It is an adorning item. It is what one makes of it that matters. What is going on in your heart, and what is the true motivation behind your choices?

There was a time in my life when I used drugs and alcohol to help me cope. I was really depressed and had a lot of emotional issues. I've been clean and sober for two years. Is it wrong for my husband to drink if he never had a drinking problem?

Many people drink because of depression. They try to fill a void or ancothetize pain. Depression runs in every human being at some level. In some, it runs deeper than in others. If your husband keeps alcohol in the house, and you are struck with a bout of depression or experience some intense emotional stress, would you really want to test yourself to see if alcohol will get a hold of your life again? Why would you risk that?

My counsel to you would be to let what's behind you stay behind you. God has granted you the grace to be free of those chains. Let them go and leave them be. Do not gamble with alcohol.

As far as your husband is concerned, if he does want a drink, it should never be in front of you where you would be put in a tempting situation. Let him know that if he chooses to have a drink, that is fine, but ask him not to drink in your presence. Ask him to keep the booze out of the house. Personally, I would suggest to him that he quit drinking too.

A husband's job is to lay down his life for his wife. If he is unable to stop drinking, then that should inform him that he has a drinking problem and needs to begin the road to recovery as well.

Certain faiths believe that wearing a cross is celebrating death. Is it wrong to wear a cross around your neck or have a tattoo with a cross?

First of all, what does it mean to you? I used to wear a cross years ago, but that was because I thought I looked cool with it. Then I got saved, and I wore the cross as a symbol that I am a Christian. So, again, I would have to ask you what it means to you.

Some people have a cross, and they kiss it and genuflect before it; they do all kinds of actions and rituals. That can lead to superstition and become unbiblical and sacrilegious.

The cross represents an event. Our Lord was nailed to a cross. He became accursed for you and me. Deuteronomy 21:23 says that everyone who hangs on a tree is cursed. Christ bore the curse of death that should have been ours. He did this so you and I might be set free from the penalty of breaking God's laws. He saved us from eternal damnation.

You will have to decide what wearing that symbol means to you, but there is nothing wrong with wearing one.

CHAPTER 8

Hell, Evil Spirits, and Demons

The pigs! In Mark 5, the Bible says that Jesus cast the demons out of a man and let them go into the pigs. The pigs ran over a cliff and drowned in the water. After the pigs drowned, where did the demons go?

Demons often possess and control specific geographic regions or areas which become their stronghold. For instance, if you read the book of Daniel, it says that for twenty-one days the prince of the

Persian kingdom withstood the angel who was dispatched to answer Daniel's prayer. The prince of the Persian kingdom was a demonic spirit that had oversight in that area.

Why is the world in the condition that it is? Why do nations do what they do? Oftentimes, there are spirits that have been assigned to a region. Paul says, "For our struggle is not against flesh and blood, but against the rulers, against the authorities, against the powers of this dark world and against the spiritual forces of evil in the heavenly realms" (Eph 6:12).

Jesus allowed the demons to go into the pigs (Matthew 8, Mark 5, and Luke 8). Once the pigs drowned, the demons either continued their descent into the abyss or searched for other hosts. Scripture does not say.

In other contexts, Jesus said that when an impure spirit comes out of a man, it goes through arid places seeking rest. It doesn't find one and returns to its original host. Finding the man clean, washed, and empty, it brings seven other demons along with it. Now, the state of that person is worse than it was before (Matthew 12:43-45; Luke 11: 24-25). Interpreters of the passage say that when people try to clean up their lives but don't fill their lives with God, Satan will eventually entrap them again. If they don't surrender and submit their lives to the Lord, they end up worse off than they were previously.

What is the lesson we can learn from this? When you are ready to change, when you start to get your act together – submit your life to Christ, be filled with the Holy Spirit, and grow in the things of God. Don't allow the enemy access to reclaim parts of your life that have been changed. If you do not fill your life and the empty places within you with the things of God, you will find yourself drawn back to the same old habits and sins. The empty space inside you is swept clean but has to be filled with something. Allow God to fill you with His Spirit, His Word, and His praise.

I have prayed and have become more sensitive and discerning to the spirit world. Whenever I am around any books or items used or about to be used in witchcraft, I get sick. Do you have any idea why this would be happening?

There are many questions we would have to ask you first. Were you once involved in the occult? Have you fully surrendered your life to Jesus Christ? How is it that you are around these books and items now?

If this is actually happening, you may still be open to those demonic spirits that can physically attach themselves to you and oppress your mind and thinking. It would be a good idea for you to make an appointment to see a pastor regarding what you are experiencing. According to 1 Corinthians 12, one of the gifts of the Holy Spirit is the discerning of spirits. It is possible that you have this gift, but we would need to talk with you and learn more about you, your background, and where you are in Christ before we can truly know what is going on.

I've been praying and reading my Bible, but what do I do when my kids see demons? I hear them and feel them sometimes. We are currently living in someone else's home.

Are the people you are living with Christians? Are you or they involved in any occult practices such as witchcraft, voodoo, Dungeons and Dragons, Ouija board, séances, etc? Is there anything going on that encourages or invites demonic activity? Demons will come where they are invited and allowed.

If the people are Christians, then you can take authority in that home. You can have pastors, elders, and men and women of God come over and anoint the house, pray over it, and take authority in the name of Jesus Christ.

If the demons have been there a long time, Jesus said they do not come out easily. They have a sense of ownership, so the struggle may require more than you are expecting; fasting and prayer may be necessary. There are some questions you want to ask your hosts and then decide what is best for you and your family. If no one in that home is open to true freedom, then you want to consider an exit plan.

Who created hell and for whom?

God created hell. It was created for the devil and his angels; the Bible says so in Matthew 25:41. Hell wasn't created for human beings. After the fall of mankind, however, hell is no longer only for the devil and his angels but is also for those who deny the grace of our Lord Jesus Christ, his resurrection from the dead, and his Lordship. It is for those who reject and refuse obedience to him. Those who reject Jesus will be cast into the lake of fire along with hell and those whose names are not found written in the Lamb's book of life.

Can a person who is filled with the Holy Spirit be affected by demonic spirits? Can a Christian be taken over?

If a person is filled with the Holy Spirit, a demonic host cannot come and dwell within the person. However, the enemy may have very solid strongholds in the person's life that have to be overcome. There are many Christians who walk around bothered, or what we call oppressed, by Satan. To say that Christians are "oppressed" means they don't know how to fight back. Satan isn't in them, but he is taking great advantage of them, especially in the mind and in broken areas of the soul. The enemy will come in wherever he can and trouble Christians. Some believers suffer from demonic oppression that has deep and long-held roots in their lives. A demon does not dwell in them, but aspects of their thinking and patterns of behavior have not been submitted to God. They have not yielded to the point of being transformed in these areas.

Psalm 23 says God restores our soul. That's why James writes that we must submit ourselves to God; resist the devil, and the devil will flee (James 4:7). It is a universal command – when we, as Christians, submit ourselves to God and resist the devil, the devil must take flight. Unfortunately, our enemy does not simply pack up his bag and walk away with a promise never to return. Satan's goal is to trap, ensnare, and destroy. He is not going to leave Christians alone. His desire is to separate us from God, and he will come at us whenever, wherever, and however he can. Submitting to God is an ongoing process. We rely on God's strength. Our strength comes in admitting and recognizing our own weaknesses and constantly and regularly submitting ourselves to God's authority.

How did Jesus combat the devil? He did so with the Word of God. I don't know how we think we can do anything less. Satan came against Jesus and said, "If you are really the Son of God, why don't you turn these stones into bread?" Jesus relied on the written Word and spoke to the devil and said, "Man does not live on bread alone but on every word that comes from the mouth of God" (see Matthew 4:1-11). Paul used the Word – calling it the sword of the Spirit (Ephesians 6:17). When the enemy comes against us, we stand on the Word of God.

Real "spiritual warfare" against the enemy is walking in truth, righteousness, faith, salvation, and prayer – all based on the Word of God; these are strategies to defeat demons.

I have heard that the devil sends his angels out to deceive everyone, including Christians. How can you tell if you're dealing with the devil's angels when they are doing a good job at deceiving?

That's a smart question. In Matthew 24, we have a glimpse of Jesus talking to his disciples about what we call end times – the time prior to his future return to earth. We call this talk the *Olivet Discourse*. Jesus said many false prophets and false teachers will come. They will be empowered by Satan and will try to deceive even the very elect – if that were possible.

The Bible instructs us to test the spirits to see whether or not they are from God, for not every spirit is from God (1 John 4:1). How do you know if a spirit is from God? Does the spirit confess Jesus as Lord? Does whatever the spirit says line up completely with the Bible?

Remember, even Satan knows how to quote Scripture. The devil quoted Scripture when he tempted Jesus. He took Jesus up to the highest point of the temple and dared, "If you are the Son of God, throw yourself down, for it is written (referring to Psalm 91), 'He will command his angels concerning you, and they will lift you up in their hands, so that you will not strike your foot against a stone'" (Matthew 4:5-6).

In response, Jesus basically said, "Yea, but I have a Scripture that trumps that (referring to Deuteronomy 6:16): 'You shall not tempt the Lord your God'" (Matthew 4:7). Jesus appropriately applied the Word of God to the devil's twisted interpretations.

Anyone can corrupt Scripture to make it mean just about anything. It is very important for every believer to learn the Word of God. God is not going to contradict Himself. Deceiving spirits come to tempt, weaken, and ultimately destroy you.

What is being said? Is it in accordance with Scripture, or is it the pretext of a verse or two taken out of context? This is where you must be careful. Almost anything can be justified by lifting a single verse out of context. Know your Word and know the character of our God. If you know your Bible and attend a godly, Bible-teaching church, it is not likely that you will be deceived.

Describe hell. Is it really bad like prison or like getting whipped all the time?

Hell or Hades (New Testament) or Sheol (Old Testament) is the place where the unsaved souls of the dead go. None of us has ever been there personally, so I will give you the Bible definition. Hell was created for the devil and his angels. It is a place of torture and torment, never ending weeping, and gnashing of teeth. Add to this the regret and remorse you will continuously experience because you heard the gospel, turned from the gospel, and got enticed by the world. Because you ran from God and spurned His love for you, you are now spending eternity in hell with the devil and his demons. It cannot possibly be an enjoyable place, nor is it some place you want to go. The jokes people make about going to hell are simply not funny. Hell is a reality.

On judgment day, even hell will be cast into the lake of fire in what is called the second death. So, yes, hell is a reality and a never-ending eternity of suffering and affliction.

CHAPTER 9

Forgiveness

If I cannot bring myself to forgive a family member for rape and molestation, does that mean I am not being obedient to God's Word? I know that God says to forgive, but what if I cannot forgive him?

Forgiveness is an act of the will, but forgiveness does not mean forgetting. What happened was wrong – it was sin. It was the grossest kind of sin. God will punish the person for his sin, and all you can really do is say, "God, I am choosing to forgive. By an act of my will, I choose to forgive." You are declaring, "I am not going to let what happened to me, or to people I know, dictate my future. I choose to forgive this man in the name of Jesus Christ." This doesn't mean you are going to be best friends with the person. It doesn't mean you are going to call him up and hang out with him, but you are going to release him from your unforgiveness and go on to live your life.

You have been bound by another person's wrongdoing for too long. It's time to heal and grow; it's time to move beyond the past and, with God's help and intervention, live in the fullness of life. Have you received any kind of counseling? If you have not already done so, I strongly recommend that you seek a qualified Christian counselor and work through the horror and pain of your past. Over time, as you heal, "forgetting" can also take place. You "forget" in the sense that the horrid actions of another person against you will not dominate or have ongoing influence over how you think, act, and live.

Forgiveness is a choice you make, but it is a choice you make only with the help of God. You cannot do it on your own. The love of Christ embraces you and is dwelling within you. You want this love to emanate from you. As negative thoughts about the person begin to come up in your mind and heart, begin to pray for him. Just pray. Ask God to heal, bless, and save the person. No, it doesn't make sense, but it is biblical. As you avail yourself to what the Holy Spirit wants to do in your life, you will be surprised at the depth of healing and love that is available to you. As you extend forgiveness, your continued healing will bring you to a place of saneness. God wants you healed and whole. In healing and wholeness you can help others. The enemy of your soul wants you stuck in anguish, bitterness, and hardness of heart toward your "enemies." You choose how you want to live.

How do I forgive a friend of many years who continuously betrays me? He is remorseful of being caught.

The Bible says we are to forgive seventy times seven a day. You say this person continuously betrays you. That's a strong statement. To betray is to cheat, to do something behind one's back, to stab in the back on purpose with malice and forethought to hurt or cause harm.

Forgive him, and get out of his way. Don't put yourself in the position to be betrayed over and over again. Since the person is your friend, you could say, "Look, I have been friends with you for a long time, and you have continually stabbed me in the back." If you have never talked to him about it, you owe him that. If you have talked to him about it, and he continues to do the same thing, you may have to say, "For my own health, I cannot emotionally, spiritually, or mentally continue to operate in this relationship." Forgive him and move on. Forgiveness also means not slandering him after you walk away. Don't talk about him and don't waste time recounting to others what he did to you. Let it be. Continue to grow in your walk with the Lord. (Now, if the person is your husband, then you two need to schedule some counseling.)

How is it that we are to forgive but not forget? How can you forgive if you are constantly reminded of somebody's wrong doing?

Who's reminding you of it? That would be the first question. Is someone reminding you of your wrong doing, or are you reminded of someone's wrong doing because he or she continues to do wrong?

If it's a situation where someone is constantly reminding you of something you did, it will never go away because the other person will keep it alive. You will have to rest in knowing that God has forgiven you even though the other person involved has not. If you have asked for forgiveness and have done everything you can to make amends, there is not much more you can do.

If this is a marriage issue, it may take some time for the offended partner to forgive, and you will have to do whatever is necessary to help your spouse see and recognize that you will not do that thing again. When trust in a marriage has been violated, it takes time and hard work to mend what's been broken. When trust has been violated, *sorry* is not enough. One's actions have to match one's words, and there must be ongoing efforts to rebuild trust. So, you can apologize, and you can say, "I'm sorry," but you will have to go above and beyond to ensure your spouse that you are repentant and trustworthy.

Maybe the subject comes up every time you two argue, or your spouse gets angry about something and brings it up. It's never going to leave you that way. It would be good for the two of you to get some sound Christian counseling.

If it's the devil bringing up the issue, and you can't seem to get it out of your mind or thinking, then you will need to spend some time praying, reading the Word, and learning what God says about forgiveness. You probably should talk to a pastor or a Christian counselor because you need someone who can help you learn to think better.

If it is a situation where someone continues to do the same wrong over and over, then it's going to be hard to forget. You will have to set appropriate boundaries so you are not continuously hurt by that person. Also, if anyone is being harmed by the person's wrong doing, then you need to get wise counsel on how to address the situation. You do not want to be a knowing party in another person's wrongdoing. If anyone else is being harmed by the person's wrongful acts, you have a responsibility to address the issue.

Please give me advice on how to bring reconciliation for my Christian family.

Someone has said that knowledge of the Word of God gives you practical, every-day wisdom. Pray and ask the Lord for wisdom. Become a peacemaker and someone who reconciles, because God has given us the ministry of reconciliation.

Where there's a lot of tension and anger, there are often deep wounds. First, speak to specific family members separately. Talking to individual family members will give you insight into long-standing issues, and you'll have greater empathy and understanding of your family's feelings. Then get the family together and let them know that you love and need them. Express to them how much it hurts your heart to see everyone at odds with each other. Be sure you have a few trustworthy brothers or sisters in Christ praying for you as you move forward. You can also speak with a pastor or an elder to get ideas and ongoing support that will guide and help you in this process.

Can a person really receive forgiveness after committing the unpardonable sin?

If it is unpardonable then, no, a person cannot be forgiven. The very word *unpardonable* means one cannot be pardoned from it.

What is the unpardonable sin? That is a tougher question. Most scholars believe it is blaspheming the Holy Spirit, and it is difficult to establish a definitive definition of exactly what that means.

Let's consider the context (Matthew 12:22-32 and Luke 12:9-11). Jesus was explaining that the work he was doing was from the Holy Spirit, but the Pharisees and religious leaders were saying his miracles were from the devil. Blaspheming the Holy Spirit seems to indicate that if you speak against the Holy Spirit or His work, then you will not be forgiven. If someone has committed the unpardonable sin, Jesus said forgiveness will not be granted in this life or in the age to come.

It's a difficult concept to fully understand. We are Pentecostals. Many people outside of our denomination believe speaking in tongues is of the devil. Would they be classified as blaspheming the Holy Spirit? They might classify us as the ones committing blasphemy.

According to Scripture, if someone truly blasphemed the Holy Spirit by committing the unpardonable sin, that person would not be forgiven. In reality, if you are really concerned about blaspheming the Holy Spirit, you won't. You have the Spirit of Christ dwelling in you. You love the Lord and are deepening your relationship with Him. Your sense of wanting to honor Him is a good safeguard against falling prey to such an unrighteous act.

Do you think someone's sins could be forgiven by someone else asking for them?

There are cases in the Old Testament where individuals prayed that God would forgive the sins of others. For instance, when the spies returned from spying out the Promised Land, the people did not want to go forward as commanded. God was prepared to destroy them, but He told Moses that He would forgive them because Moses had asked Him to forgive them. God said he would forgive them, but they would die in the desert; they would not enter the Promised Land (Numbers 14).

In other instances, Samuel prayed for the forgiveness of the people (1 Samuel 7 and 12), Daniel prayed for the nation of Israel to be forgiven (Daniel 9), and Abraham prayed for King Abimelech to be forgiven (Genesis 20).

Christ came and made a way for all of us, each and every one of us, to pray directly to the Father for forgiveness. Through Jesus Christ, we have access to God regardless of rank, education, social standing, ethnicity, or anything else. "If we confess our sins, he is faithful and just and will forgive us our sins and purify us from all unrighteousness" (1 John 1:9).

We can ask God to forgive others. We can ask God to help them recognize their sin, and we can ask Him to draw them to Himself. We can ask God to extend His forgiveness to repentant hearts. In the end, each individual must confess his or her own sins and repent before the Lord.

When I say my prayers at night, is it right for me to ask God for forgiveness of the sins that I have committed throughout the day, if I then turn around and commit the same sins all over again the next day?

God is faithful and just. When we confess our sins, he forgives us. He cleanses us of unrighteousness (1 John 1:9). It sounds as though you are truly grieved about the sin you are committing; however, you are not taking any steps to stop sinning. Change can only occur through submission and obedience to the Holy Spirit and the Word of God. Please read Galatians 5:16-26.

Are you repentant? A repentant heart says, "God, I have committed this sin, but I am making a decision and a commitment to turn from it and focus in a new direction. Teach me a new response." Whether the sin is anger or gossip or lust or whatever, ask the Lord to teach you another way to react and respond, so you don't have to keep coming to Him and asking Him for forgiveness of the same sin over and over again.

You may be "hooked" in a habit. Each night you ask the Lord to forgive you, but you are unwilling, and very possibly unable, to do what is necessary to move toward healing. If that is the case, do you really mean it when you say you are sorry and you ask for forgiveness? Are you sorry? Are you sorry enough to begin to do things differently? Are you sorry enough to get help?

Repentance means to turn around – to move in the other direction. When you are ensnared in a sin, repentance often requires getting help and taking active steps to stop sinning. A year from now, do you want to be stuck in the same sin?

Maybe you have tried and tried to change, and you simply cannot do it. You have failed and failed again. Admitting that you are powerless over this sin is the first step in moving in a new direction. You cannot conquer it on your own. You need God's help! Attending *Celebrate Recovery* would be a good place for you to begin exploring what is going on inside you that disables you from breaking free and living in wholeness. *(Celebrate Recovery* meets weekly at our church. You can also look them up online for a meeting near you – *http://www.celebraterecovery.com).*

The Lord will forgive you; however, do not continue thinking, "*It's okay if I sin again because God will forgive me.*" It's not okay to have such a presumptuous attitude. Some people commit the same sins again and again and then go to daily confession in an absurd pattern of spiritual game playing. If you are serious about wanting to change, prove it by seeking help. Stop telling yourself, "*This is the last time I will do this thing. I won't commit this sin anymore.*" How many years have you told yourself the same lies? Think about it – If you don't begin to do something differently, you cannot expect different results.

How do I know if God has forgiven me for ending pregnancies in the past? How can I become a strong mother, both mentally and spiritually, for my children?

If you have confessed your sin, the Bible says God has already forgiven you. All you have done and then have confessed is covered under the Blood of Christ.

Abortion is a serious matter. It is the taking of a life, and it affects the mother, and sometimes the father, beyond what most people talk about or what many of us could ever imagine. When you make the decision to abort a child, you don't realize the psychological agony you are likely to experience for years after the procedure.

The mental anguish that many women experience following an abortion can be crippling. We are so very sorry that you've had to endure so much pain. The grief and regret you've felt is not abnormal. At the same time, God does not want you to live the rest of your life in guilt and anguish. At some point you have to stop beating yourself up. You cannot change the past, so please stop living in it. You have accepted Christ. You have asked God to forgive you. Your sins have been forgiven – even the sin of abortion. Hear me on this – God has forgiven you for terminating your pregnancies. You will see those children in heaven.

Face today and be the best mom you can be. Your heart may always long for those children. You cannot change the past, but you can make up your mind that, with the Lord's help, you are going to go forward as a new creation, guided by His Word and choosing His ways. Let what has happened help you be a better, stronger, more caring and compassionate person. Let it help set your compass toward being a better mother, not out of guilt, but out of an understanding that your children are precious gifts and are only yours for a short while. Learn to laugh with your kids and appreciate them for the amazing individuals they are. Today is what you have, so make the most of it.

If you need help in being a better parent, help is available. There are support groups, teachings, books, Bible studies, etc. Reach out and bring others into your circle.

Pastor, I had an abortion years ago. I still feel awful. I know God has forgiven me, but how do I forgive myself?

Please open your Bible to the passage that says, "Forgive yourself, and you will be forgiven." Oh, wait, that's not in the Bible, is it? God is the only one who can forgive. Jesus Christ died on a cross. He paid the penalty for sin for all mankind. He died that we might be forgiven. We are made righteous by his blood and his blood alone. God forgives us because Christ already paid the price for our sin. The issue may not be that you cannot forgive yourself. Perhaps the issue is that you are presently unable to accept that if you confess your sins, Father God forgives you.

My dear, you are forgiven. The Creator of heaven and earth beckons with arms open to hold you close to Himself. He wants to wrap you in His arms of mercy and love. Why do you stand so far off, thinking that forgiveness is in your power? That's your pride talking. You are not God. Forgiveness is not based on your forgiving yourself.

You are accepted in the Beloved. Accept his gift of grace.

We cannot clean ourselves up. We cannot make ourselves righteous before God – God alone forgives.

Recognize that you are human, weak, and frail. You had an abortion – you messed up. You messed up big time. But that's why Christ died – because we have all messed up. We are all filthy sinners.

God forgives you. Can you accept that?

You are forgiven. It's time to live.

If you would like some emotional support in dealing with the pain and regret of having an abortion and would like to speak with a competent Christian counselor, we have a number of ladies at our church who have been trained in post-abortion counseling who can talk with you.

Please call us and let us help you.

Call the church office at 510-357-5723, extension 104, and we will put you in contact with one of these Christian sisters. Please reach out to someone who can walk with you through the healing process.

CHAPTER 10

Homosexuality

Do you concur with the recent rulings about same-sex marriage?

I discuss this in my book, *Let's Get the Gay Thing Straight.* There are about fifteen to twenty men in my life that I love. I would die for them, and I believe they would give their lives for me. That does not mean that I have to have sex with them. You can love someone without having sex with him or her.

If you want to be biblical, and we don't have to be – we can just share personal opinions – but if you want me to be biblical, then I have to tell you that same-sex marriage is not God's plan for us. As Jesus said, "In the beginning… a man and a woman… and the two shall become one flesh. And what God has joined together, let man not separate" (Matthew 19:4-6). I cannot agree with gay marriage. I cannot, unless you just want an opinion. This is not a popular stance. It will invoke the ire of many, even some who consider themselves believers. It will invite cries of intolerance and condemnation, but I have an obligation to God and to the congregation I pastor to present a biblical view on this issue.

When we take a biblical stance, we become a target for persecution, but that is to be expected. You see, nations established their own ways and laws. Men and women raised their fists to heaven and said, "This is how we are going to live, and we don't care how *You* (God) tell us to live." Jesus came on the scene and began telling people what was right and what was wrong, and they responded, "Who are you to tell us?"

If you do not want to be biblical, fine. An unbiblical course with a humanistic worldview is the direction our nation has chosen. Why? We have become a nation of leaders and individuals who are not trying to follow God's ways. God's ways are not popular. He has established what is right and what is wrong, but mankind chooses to go against God's laws. It's human nature to rebel. We don't want to be told what we can and cannot do. As far as our country is concerned, if people are not following God's ways, then it is just a matter of flipping a coin every time new leadership comes into power. Every time we get a new regime of leadership, the leaders are going to alter the rules. At some point though, if we are ever going to be one nation under God, we must understand what that really means: We are under God, not over God. It means we are under God's authority and His will and, if that is the case, we have to be godly.

Being biblical is important for us as believers.

Persecution comes when you take such a stance, so be prepared. Still, it does not mean we do not love. It does not mean we hate. We love, and we respond in love. We do not withhold love from individuals who have chosen a homosexual lifestyle. We simply take a biblical stance in all situations, including same-sex marriage.

I know a lesbian couple who were recently recognized as a "married" couple. I want to invite them to church, but they don't know if they want to come because they say they love the Lord and are going to stay together and stay married. What should I say? They are very important people in my life.

I would begin very gently and non-aggressively. They love the Lord, so remind them that the Lord instituted the church. Invite them to come, sit, listen and, just like with every other topic and with every other sermon, weigh out what the preacher is saying. Is it really the Word of God? Is Scripture rightly divided (accurately taught)? If so, then they have to take it in and apply it to their lives.

Simply extend the invitation to them to come. They do not have to be afraid to come into the house of the Lord. Continue to pray for them and be a part of their lives.

God never said we can come to Him on our terms. He is God. Jesus said, "If you love me, you will obey my teaching" (John 14:23). A comparison would be two unmarried heterosexual people living together. They say they love the Lord and call themselves devout Christians, but what does God's Word say about such behavior? We don't pick and choose which Scriptures we will obey. According to 1 Corinthians 5:11, if this heterosexual couple took the same stance as your two friends, Paul says we are not even to share a meal with them. Because God is a merciful God, we forget that He has standards, and He calls His children to grow in the character of Christ. Just saying "I'm a Christian" does not mean I really am one or that what I'm doing is pleasing to God.

Invite your friends to church and allow the Holy Spirit to do His work.

If I am free to choose, then why can't I choose to be gay?

You can choose to do whatever you want to do. Does that mean that what you choose to do is what God wants you to do? God has given you the ultimate responsibility of being a free human being. He will let you do whatever you want to do.

He gives us free choice. It's one of the reasons people love God so much. It is also the reason so many people do not love Him. On the one hand, they want a God who is all loving and stops all evil in the world. On the other hand, they do not want anyone, including this God, telling them what to do (or not to do) or setting up any parameters for their lives.

God does not force Himself on any of us. He has given us the option and the ability to choose how we will live. We can choose to live for Him, or we can choose to live against Him.

In your question, are you asking, "If we're free to choose, why can't I choose to do wrong?" Remember that you can. You are free to live as you wish. You can choose to live according to your own ideas or to society's ideas of right and wrong, or you can choose to live according to God's standards of right and wrong as communicated through His Word, the Bible.

So, if you are free to choose God's direction for your life, then you will take the time to find out what He wants. As a believer, you want God's will for your life. Life will not be perfect, and you will not always get what you want when you want it, but you will have full peace and joy and blessing. Nothing compares to that.

In your choosing, choose God's way. You simply cannot go wrong. You might want to get a copy of my book *Let's Get the Gay Thing Straight*. I believe it will speak to some of the conflict you may be experiencing.

CHAPTER 11

Marriage and Sex

My husband and I are separated. He is living with his girlfriend and was never really the best husband; however, you have been preaching so much about forgiveness, and he is asking to be forgiven now. What should I do? I do love him very much, but I don't trust him. Do I forgive him and take him back?

What should you do? I think the very fact that you are asking the question says that you are open to forgiveness. If you weren't open, you wouldn't even ask. I would put some stipulations on your husband very quickly.

Let's call him Bob for right now. If he wants to come home, here is what you have to tell him: *"Listen, Bob, you really expect me to take you back? Okay, here is what has to happen before we can move forward. You go in and see one of the pastors. Also, you absolutely and one hundred percent cut off all contact with this woman. That means no phone, no text, no email, no Youtube or Facebook or Twitter; nothing! There must be no communication with her at all. If you can start with those conditions, that would be a beginning for us, and I will consider repairing this marriage. However, if you cannot cut off all contact with this person, one hundred percent, just tell me right now because then we're done. If you are not willing to commit to ongoing counseling, we're done."*

Asking for your forgiveness is one thing, but your husband also has to be willing to work on his issues and work on the marriage with you. Give him the opportunity. The rest is up to him. You move forward from there. If he chooses not to do these things, then you grieve the marriage you'd always hoped for and continue the work of forgiving him and getting on with your life.

I am married to a wonderful Christian man; however, I am lonely. I feel a past issue has not been laid to rest. I love him dearly, but I feel so alone every day. I want to have those deep loving feelings that we once had for each other. How can we regain our love without resurfacing our past and move forward into a beautiful, godly future with each other?

You move forward by doing just that: You begin to move forward. It sounds like there is something from the past that has not been forgiven. It surely is not forgotten. I have to read a bit into the question because I am not exactly sure what is going on. It sounds like one of you did something; one of you violated something in the relationship. It sounds like the offended party is using that as a control mechanism or is unable to move past it.

Let me speak to the offended partner for a moment. You who were offended, you control the relationship because you bring that subject up any time you want by saying, "Yea, what about the time you..." or "Well, remember when you..." Who can live under that? You are determining how close your partner can get, and your spouse wants to get close again.

Invite some wise counselors into your lives. Maybe you can talk to an older married couple or come in for counseling. Most certainly, pray. Healing can take place, but you both have to open up and allow it. Moving beyond the past when someone has been wounded or trust has been violated can seem daunting, but healing and growth can occur if both parties are truly open and are willing to do the necessary work to make it happen.

I am married and fighting the desire of my flesh. How do I overcome? Help!

I don't know what you are fighting, so I am going to have to assume. You are married and are fighting the desire of the flesh to cheat, to look at pornography, to lust? Are you being tempted by somebody? You ask how to fight the desire of your flesh. You already know the answer to your question – you fight the desire. You stay accountable to persons of the same sex who love the Lord. You get some counsel, and you figure out why you are feeling this way. The more you allow yourself to "feel" overwhelmed by the desire, the more power the desire has over you.

Get help! Find out what can be done in the marriage to rectify the situation. Learn how to connect with your mate on a vulnerable and sincere level. Let's get to the root of your issues and get healed once and for all and not just put a tiny bandage on it.

I do have some news for you, though. We are all fighting the desires of the flesh; it's a part of being human. However, believe it or not, you do not have to give in to temptation.

Is it sinful for me to put a stripper pole in our bedroom? My husband and I are happily married, and we've never cheated on each other. There have been no issues with porn. We just want to spice things up a bit.

What a husband and wife do in the privacy of their own bodroom is between them; however, there should never be a third person or porn of any kind or anything which would lead you and your spouse into temptation and sin. If you are both saved and are okay with a pole in the room, then that's up to you.

I wonder how many married men reading this would say to their wives "Girl, PUT the pole in the room!"

That's all I'm going to say.

Marriage is a covenant. Are atheists, agnostics, and the unsaved in a covenant relationship when they marry, or are they exempt because they are ignorant of the covenant principle?

When you go before the judge or the priest or the pastor and get married, God honors it, and it is a viable marriage. I once heard someone say that if someone is not saved, or if both are not saved, the marriage really is not a marriage that is "blessed" by God. I disagree with that. When Jesus spoke of marriage in Matthew 5 and Matthew 19, he was speaking to the multitudes, and not all of them were necessarily under God's covenant.

When a man and woman get married by law, when they marry legally – they are married. God wants them to remain in the "covenant" of marriage because that is the commitment they made to love each other.

My husband and I have some very serious issues in our marriage. We need to make an appointment to see you. My husband thinks he should talk to you first, alone. I have mixed feelings about this. What do you think?

I have no problem with one of you coming in first. Just make an agreement that the other gets to come in alone as well. The Scriptures say that only a fool makes a decision after hearing one side of a story. I'll listen well and wait to hear what the other partner has to say. After that we will all come together and work things out between you.

How do you move on when you get a divorce? I am in so much pain.

Divorce is a very painful thing. There is a mystery when you get married that the world doesn't truly understand. Two people enter the union as two but become one. A divorce tears that "one" back into two. It's incredibly painful and can be painful for many years afterward. You must allow God to heal you and move you forward. It is not an easy process, but healing can happen. Having someone to talk to who is of the same gender and is competent and spiritually mature can help you. Attending a divorce recovery group would be a good start in the healing process. Also, do not make the mistake of getting involved with someone physically or emotionally because you feel sad or lonely.

Is there any possible chance that the broken marriage can be restored? Remember, divorce does not end a marriage, remarriage to a new person does.

What does God say about remarriage if your mate is deceased?

Please see 1 Corinthians 7 and Romans 7. Both talk about marriage after the death of a spouse. You are perfectly allowed to remarry if you want to. The Apostle Paul does set some guidelines and says your new partner must be someone who is in Christ. You are not doing anything wrong by remarrying, but the marriage must be to a believer.

Paul also says that you would probably be better off single. That was his preference and suggestion; however, it is not a command from the Lord. Some folks enjoy the single life and simply focus their time and attention on God. Others want to live out the remainder of their days with a loving spouse. You choose.

I signed a domestic partnership some time ago with my boyfriend. What is the church's stance on such agreements?

If you signed a domestic partnership, why didn't you just go ahead and get married? A domestic partnership is man made. Marriage is God made. If both of you are believers, or if one of you is a believer, you are compromising your faith in coming together in this manner. You are not married, and you are living together. Where is the wisdom in that? Where is the faith in that? I advise you to get some solid Christian counseling. If you attend Faith Fellowship, come in and talk to Pastor Vince or to me, and let us help you through this situation. Let's see if we can get you both to a better place. If you attend church elsewhere, please speak with your pastor. A domestic partnership is not a marriage. If you are believers, your current relationship is not in accordance with God's Word.

Are your spouse and children automatically covered by the grace of God if they are unsaved? What else can you do other than pray for them?

According to 1 Corinthians 7, Paul does say that an unbeliever is covered while married to a believer, but that doesn't mean the unbeliever is saved. It means the unbelieving spouse and the children are under God's umbrella of protection and grace because of the believer. Ultimately, however, every individual has to make his or her own decision to accept Jesus Christ as Lord and Savior.

Your heart must ache for your loved ones. Be careful how you express your concern. If you are a female, besides praying for them, rather than preaching to them and trying to win them with words, which drives them further away, let it be your gentle and quiet spirit, your calm demeanor, and your reverent heart towards your husband that attracts them to the Lord (see 1 Peter 3). Remember, Sarah called Abram "my lord." Maybe you should try calling your spouse "my lord." Okay, maybe not. But you get my point.

Your family tunes out the nagging and the preaching. Love them, know them deeply as individuals, and pray for them. It's not your job to "get them saved." That's God's work. Shine Christ's love within your home. Leave the rest up to God.

Is there really no sex in heaven?

The Bible says that at the resurrection, people will neither marry nor be given in marriage. It states that we will be like the angels in heaven (Matthew 22:30) and seems to imply that we will be sexless beings, neither experiencing sexual stimulation nor desiring sexual gratification. Right now, that may seem impossible for you to even imagine because we are currently limited by human thinking in bodies as we know them. Eternity is beyond our limited understanding.

I don't have a question, but a comment. I know you encourage us to make marriages work and not to give up on our marriage, but some marriages should not have taken place. It is difficult for those of us who did try everything but realized that, in the end, it was best to walk away. We need encouragement too, Pastor.

I feel your pain, and I am so very sorry for all the hurt you have suffered. I also think that with the right tools and sufficient work, and if you have two willing people, just about any marriage can be healed. Both parties have to be prepared to endure the tough work required to mend what has been broken. It takes only one person to cause a break, but if you have two people who are willing to bridge the divide, then work can be done.

Even though you say you tried everything, the reality is you may not have tried everything because everything that you know is not everything there is to know. There is more you may need to learn. I'm not saying that some marriages shouldn't have ended. Maybe there were affairs or one person couldn't give up an addiction and was destroying the family. Maybe there was abuse or abandonment. Maybe that's just the way it was because one person or the other became hard hearted.

If both people are open, a marriage can be healed. If it did not work for you, my heart goes out to you. I pray that you will obey the will of God and follow His steps very, very closely from here on out.

As a Christian trying to be with God, how do you stay with the person you married when that person does not love God and does not care about the things of God?

Read 1 Corinthians 7 very slowly and very carefully. I think you can read it for yourself, and you will see that it holds a very legitimate answer to your question. If you treat your spouse lovingly, and your spouse treats you well, the marriage can maintain a certain level of harmony even though your spouse does not share this important aspect of your life with you. You are responsible for your own faith. Your spouse's actions are not yours. Do not preach or become dogmatic. Do not try to force your beliefs on your husband or wife. Love and honor God and continue to pray for your mate. Do not expect your spouse to live according to God's standards when he or she does not know the Lord. If you sincerely live as a loving partner, and there still is no peace, let the Word of God direct you. Also read 1 Peter 3:1-7.

I know the Bible says that we are not to have sex before marriage, but what if you get married and do not have sex with each other? My spouse and I do not seem to be sexually compatible.

You and your spouse can learn to be good lovers to each other by learning to meet each other's needs. First, both of you should see a doctor and find out if there are any medical problems impairing your intimacy. Are there any possible physical concerns such as thyroid issues, lack of testosterone in the male, lack of estrogen in the female, or maybe some other condition? High blood pressure can be a factor. Are either of you taking medication for high blood pressure? Any number of medical conditions can play a part in diminishing your lovemaking.

Next, are you and your spouse each comfortable with your own bodies, or is there extreme self consciousness due to size or shape or body image? Sometimes one party feels overly self conscious and believes the spouse is focused on every flaw and imperfection. This greatly inhibits full sexual freedom between married couples.

Are there any emotional issues from the past such as childhood sexual trauma or abuse? Left unaddressed, childhood sexual abuse has the potential to destroy your love life. If there was sexual abuse in the past, it's very important to have some heartfelt conversations with each other and get into counseling.

Now, it is also possible that one of you is being selfish and is not considering the other in lovemaking. Have you taken the time to find out each other's likes and dislikes? Are you able to talk honestly to each other about these things?

I'd also have to ask whether either of you is addicted to pornography. Pornography is a consuming stronghold that is very difficult to break. When a person (usually the male, but not always) gets hooked on porn, sexual gratification becomes an isolating experience, and the person often loses touch with how to properly communicate sexually with his (or her) spouse. If this is the case, you must get help immediately. Some people will say that looking at pornography is just what men do. It is not what men of God are meant to do or have to do. It is very hurtful toward your spouse and damaging to your relationship with each other.

If either of you feels that your sex together is not good, then you owe it to each other to seek medical help and/or counseling to figure out what is going on because the Bible says it is your rightful duty to meet the sexual needs of your spouse. You are not to withhold from each other except by mutual agreement for a season of prayer and then come back together again so that Satan does not tempt you to seek gratification outside of your marriage.

Again, anyone can be a good lover, but you have to be willing to learn the needs of your spouse. Communication with each other, with God, and with a counselor can help you do that. In the meantime, do what you can to help your mate feel safe with you. Let your actions demonstrate that you can be trusted with your mate's body, heart, and deepest feelings.

I am currently married to a guy who is in prison for life. My family doesn't know. I know that if I tell them, it will break their hearts. But I don't want to have to choose between him and them. What shall I do? My family may disown me if they find out.

You've gotten yourself into quite a difficult situation. You already made a choice between this man and your family when you married him. You knew when you wedded yourself to him that you were going to have to live a covert life. You knew that your family wasn't going to be pleased with your decision.

If I were you, I would give my family a chance. I would sit down with them and humble myself. I would say, "Listen, I did something that I knew you wouldn't approve of, but I already made the decision. I got married. I married a guy, and he's in prison for life. Please do not disown me. More than ever, I need your love and support. I need you to prayerfully help me walk through this. I need help knowing what to do going forward in my life and in this marriage."

I would take a chance on the family because you kind of forced the situation, and you need your family in your life. You have made a decision that will affect your entire future. You bound yourself to someone who may not see outside prison walls for the rest of his life and yours. That is going to have a profound effect on the remainder of your life, and it's not a road that you will be able to walk alone.

The previous question breaks my heart. The young lady who submitted this question obviously felt she was very much in love with this man – so much so that she married him. We hope that with God's help and with the support of family and friends, she will live a fulfilled life with a man she rarely gets to see.

I'd like to take a moment to address the single men and women. Singles, be wise in your dating and marriage choices. Listen to people who know and love you. Make friends with mature believers and welcome them into your life and your world. The decision to marry is one of the most important decisions you will ever make in your life. Do not make the decision hastily or in isolation. Your family, your friends, your pastors and church leaders are a network of people who care about you and want the best for you. Take the time to allow others into your private world and trust their guidance.

Many singles desire to be married, and marriage is sanctioned by God. It is a life-long commitment and is the ultimate covenant between a man and a woman. Love is wonderful – but as you can see from the questions in this chapter, real love goes far beyond the "feelings" of love. Real love is not always easy. Marriage is not easy. Marriage is not made of the fairytale romances you see portrayed in movies and storybooks. Loving another person takes conscious acts of your will and determination of heart and spirit to remain steadfast, faithful, and kind. It is hard work but, if you are willing, it is well worth the time and effort required to have a lasting, God-honoring, "until death do us part" relationship.

CHAPTER 12

Single and Saved
(and no sex)

What does it mean to be actively single? Please be specific.

I am not sure what your definition of "actively single" might be. In my mind, "actively single" means you are single, and you are living your life. You are getting out of the house, and you're experiencing life. You're doing things; you are not just sitting around the house "waiting" all the time. That could be one definition.

Actively single could mean you are dating a lot. If you are dating a lot, I would hope that it is with the utmost honor and with the understanding that the relationships are purely platonic. If not, I would question your integrity. Why would you go from one guy to another or from one lady to another? There should be truthfulness and integrity in pursuing members of the opposite sex. We don't foolishly or deceitfully commit ourselves to multiple people at once. Believers don't act like that. It's okay to go out for coffee or go to public places for dinner or activities, but Christians should have a different value system than the world.

Here is a thought on how to be actively single: Pursue God and develop and use the gifts He has given you you. What are your gifts? Steward those gifts for His glory. Use and grow in those gifts. Get training, get education, and get experience. What are your passions in life? Be "actively single" in that you are on-fire for Jesus and filling your life with activities that fulfill your life passions, benefit others, and bring glory to God.

If you want to meet members of the opposite sex, get involved in church activities. Go to Christian functions and spend time with people who follow God. What kinds of things do you enjoy doing? If you like clubbing, do you really believe you will meet the man or woman of your dreams at a nightclub? Really? What man or woman who truly loves the Lord and is serving Him is going to spend his or her evenings drinking the night away entwined with strangers on the danoo floor?

What God-honoring, uplifting things do you enjoy doing? Be "actively single" by getting up and out of your front door. Get out of "waiting" mode and into "being and doing" mode.

How can singles live a fulfilled life in the process of waiting for God?

You live a fulfilled life by doing exactly that – living a fulfilled life. What are you waiting for? Are you waiting for life to begin when you get married? Life is happening right now; whether you choose to participate in it or not is up to you. I hope you choose to live.

I was a single man for a number of years before I got married, and I had a great time. I was not involved in all kinds of sin, and I was not dating all kinds of people. I was living my life. If you want to be biblical about it, spend the bulk of your time serving the Lord. Use your time wisely by doing profitable things. Now would be the time to take some trips, go on vacations, take classes, and explore opportunities. When that special man or woman comes along, your time will no longer be your own, and there may not be much money to spare. Then when babies come along, you will enter yet another season. You may never again have the freedom that you have now.

Get out there; meet other on-fire Christian singles. Do what is right before God. Allow yourself to have some fun, mingle, and travel. Above all, let God use you. 1 Corinthians 7 says that a single person can devote himself/herself fully to the Lord, while married people have to split their devotion between serving God and pleasing a spouse.

137

So many singles think life will begin when they meet that special someone. Life – married or single – is happening right now.

If two people are in a relationship, do you feel that a guy should pay for everything? Why or why not?

I think that in our day and age, with both sexes out in the work place, the responsibility can be shared if that is your preference. It wasn't always that way. There was a time when the men went to work, and many women stayed home and took care of the children. So, of course, the man paid for everything because he made the money. We are not in that kind of society any more. Men and women both work.

In the dating world, some men still like to pay for everything. They are showing that they are able to provide for a woman. Other couples, sometimes out of necessity, prefer to share the financial responsibilities of the dating relationship.

Either way, ladies, if you are single, the man needs to show you chivalry. What does that mean? He should open doors for you; he should pull out your chair and treat you politely. He should talk to you respectfully. He should not expect physical affection because he has taken you to dinner. Please don't fall for that.

If the two of you are not in a dating relationship and are just exploring the possibility by going out on a date, then a man should be a man and pay for the dating event. If, however, the female works and wants to pitch in, there is no problem with that.

If you are in a serious relationship, talk about the money issue and decide how the two of you want to handle this subject going forward.

If God is love, and we sin every day, why is sex before marriage one that He can't forgive if you continue in it?

First, please be careful of quoting the Bible without really quoting the Bible. There is also more to this question. Listen, God can forgive you. Your sin is not greater than His love and grace; however, a few things are set in motion if you are going to continue in behavior that is contrary to His Word. Number one, it is blatant sin. Number two, you are creating a soul tie with an individual who is not your spouse. Number three, you might get a disease; and number four, you are selling yourself short. Why are you sleeping with someone you are not married to?

As we tell all the singles, the Bible says that all other sins are outside the body, but he who sins sexually, sins against his own body (1 Corinthians 6:18-20). There is something that happens at a very deep spiritual level when you continue to sin sexually.

God created sex. It is a good and beautiful creation, and it has a purpose. What is the purpose of sex? It is for married couples – for procreation and for pleasure. Couples renew their vows every time they come together physically. Any other reason besides that is really a perversion that the enemy and the world have brought into what is meant to be shared solely within the covenant relationship.

If you are sexually sinning, stop. Stop! There is a deeper issue going on within you, and you have to find out why you are giving yourself away so freely and without commitment. Do you believe no one would ever want to marry you? That's a lie. Are you afraid of commitment because your heart has been broken, so you don't trust the opposite sex anymore and consistently settle for less than what God intended? You may need some counseling so that you can receive healing and wholeness from the Lord.

Yes, God can and does forgive sexual sin, but the effects of sin can last a while – sometimes a lifetime and beyond to future generations. Often when we go against God's Word, we think the effect is only on ourselves. We don't stop to consider the consequences our actions may have on our children (born or yet unborn) and on the lives that will follow us. It's a sobering thought to consider.

Would it be okay to be with an unbeliever because the believers treat you worse than an unbeliever? If God loves everyone equally, can't we too?

Do you see how you are working your way around issues here? Are you trying to rationalize your way into a relationship with some unsaved guy who treats you a little better than some of the Christian guys you have dated? Some of the Christian guys you dated were probably losers. No, it is not okay for you to join yourself with an unbeliever. The Bible clearly instructs you as a believer not to tie yourself to an unbeliever in a covenant relationship (see 2 Corinthians 6:14-18). Find a believing winner.

Singles, take time to get to know the people of the opposite sex who say they are Christians. Just because you see him at church from time to time does not mean the man is living saved. Just because she sings in the choir does not mean the woman is ready for a mature relationship. Simply because a person calls himself or herself a Christian does not mean that he or she is a true believer or a mature one. Use discernment in deciding to pursue someone. If it's truly your heart's desire to be married, then there is a good Christian partner in God's plan for your life.

As a single Christian woman, what qualities do I need to look for in a potential husband?

Some women believe a future partner must be tall, rich, and good looking. That's the world's system, isn't it? Others believe he must be a man of God, honest, a leader, and he must have a job.

How about self control? I had a woman tell me recently that she had met someone and was wondering if she should put him in a tempting situation to find out if he was a man of God or not. Well, that is not a very godly thing to do, and it's very foolish. Men of God get weak too. Don't deliberately tantalize him. And if you are intentionally enticing him, what does that say about you? You don't want to put him in a tempting situation; you want to try *not* to put him in a tempting situation. Now, if you are not putting him in a tempting situation, and he still tries to make a move on you, drop him and drop him quickly. Do not waver in this decision, and do not date him again.

If he is such a great catch, how come he isn't caught? Can we ask his last three girlfriends why they didn't catch him? You might be surprised. Are there issues in his life that need resolution before he enters a serious relationship? Does he acknowledge his issues, and has he begun working on them? Do you know his pastor? Who does he hang out with? These are things to consider before eyeing someone and telling your friends, "He's the one!"

How do you determine when it is God putting a man in your life? I am a single mother who was physically and mentally abused. I have a hard time knowing if it is time to accept a man into my life.

The first thing you need to do is get into counseling. Get with a pastor or Christian counselor so you can work through the lingering issues of the abuse. The man who is going to be your husband is going to have to pay the tab for what you have previously suffered. You can think you are healed, but that healing won't be tested until you are in a serious relationship.

Once you are in that relationship, your man will have to love you through some of the deep issues of your heart. He is also going to need some counsel because he probably won't know how to walk with you through the healing process. He will have to learn how to respond to you and act toward you in sensitive situations. He is going to have to gain the skills to maneuver with you through and around the "triggers" in your life. That is a process that will take some time.

Find a man who is committed to serving the Lord and is willing to learn *how* to love you.

How do you question a man's walk with the Lord, and should you? How do you know if he truly walks with the Lord?

This question sounds like it is coming from a female asking about a guy she is interested in. What do you look for? Observe his behavior over a two to four month period of time. Time will tell. Listen to what he does and doesn't say; watch what he does and doesn't do. You will begin to have a fairly solid idea of who he is. Find out where has he been, and who his pastor has been. Who knows him? There are ways to learn more about people. Don't just jump for him because you are attracted to him. Pray and ask the Holy Spirit to reveal the truth to you. The Holy Spirit will always reveal truth. He will reveal things to let you know if it is not God's will for you to be involved in this relationship; however, you must be willing to heed His leadings and His warnings. Sometimes we are so head over heels over someone, we ignore the signs. We often rely on feelings first, then regret it later. There are many wolves in sheep's clothing. Be wise.

How can you know, without a shadow of a doubt, whether a particular man is right for you?

Here is a litmus test. First, is he saved and accountable to someone? Second, does he have a job? Number three, is he wanting and willing to honor and protect your integrity by not kissing you or persuading (convincing, cajoling, begging) you to be sexually active? You are a woman of God. You want to date in a way that honors the Lord, and getting to know a man will take some time. Allow trustworthy friends to have a voice in the situation. At least hear what they have to say and why they are saying it. If your friends really know you and love you, they will be honest with you because they care about your spiritual well being. Next, talk to your pastors. Let your pastors meet him and talk with him and ask him some questions. Then, if he is right for you, you will know it; God will approve it, and it will be great. You can get married... and then the trouble will start.

How long is too long to date without a proposal? I'm praying and waiting on God.

No, you're not. You're waiting on that man; that is, of course, if you are female. But just in case this question is from a guy, let's look at the issue from both perspectives. Assuming that you are female, remember that old saying, "No sense buying the cow if he's getting the milk for free"? First and foremost, make sure that you are not sexually involved with him. You need to ask him, "What are your plans? Do you want to spend the rest of your life with me or not?" You don't have to phrase it that way but, ladies, you do have to know that after dating someone for a while, it's okay to talk about the future of a relationship. If the two of you have been dating exclusively for a few months, it's time to have a conversation. Some women hang on for years... just waiting. They say, "I don't want to make waves. I don't want to direct the relationship." You won't be directing the relationship, and you won't be pursuing him. However, the man may need a wake-up call. If you want to just keep waiting and waiting, that is up to you; but while you are waiting, you are keeping yourself from some other good men out there who may be very interested in you.

Now it could be a man asking this question. Dude, what are you waiting on? What is the hang-up here? How long have you been dating? Let the woman know you want to spend the rest of your life with her. If she is hesitant, ask her, "What are your plans?" You have to let her know that you are not going to hang around forever. At the same time, if you are the hesitant one, is that really fair to her? Are you waiting and waiting because you fear commitment? Are you thinking that someone "better" might come along? It's time to grow up, be a man, and make a decision. She is waiting for you to take the lead. If you take a chance, and she declines your offer, then better to know now than ten years down the road after the two of you have invested years of your lives... waiting.

I asked God to take my most significant other away if he was not the right person for me. Why does it hurt so much to let him go?

Sometimes we have to go through the pain of a right decision to get the best result.

You were dating someone, and you had some serious reservations about him. Yes, it hurts to let him go. You've already given your heart to that person and are probably in love with him, but there is a part of you that knows that he is not the best thing for you. If you know he's not right for you, and you know it's not the relationship God wants for you, let him go. You will get over him. Those are difficult words for you to hear right now, but you have to trust God on this one.

Give yourself some time. The pain will ease and you will move on. You will love again.

What is the best way to get over a breakup and mend a broken heart? I am a new believer and I do not know what to do.

New believer or an old one, a human heart is a human heart – when it breaks, it hurts. The reason you hurt is because the relationship meant something to you. You hurt because you cared about someone, and a part of you still cares. When your heart is hurting, there is no instant fix. The Holy Spirit will take you through a process of healing, and you must give yourself time to heal.

For a new believer, remember, God wants your full attention. Sometimes things happen in our lives that push us into the Lord's arms. We don't understand how or why certain situations turn out the way they do, but these difficult circumstances draw us closer to God. Now that this relationship has ended, run to God. Find solace in Him. He will teach you some things. This is a time for you to learn to trust God at a deeper level.

When you have a broken heart, you can do one of two things. You can grow closer to God, or you can move away from Him. Heartache allows you to trust God and set a better standard for your life and your relationships. The other choice is that you will become angry and foolish, and you'll set a standard of blaming others and distancing yourself from God. Don't do the latter. When you are going through a tough zone – and everybody goes through them – get closer to God, not farther away. The natural instinct may be to run from God, but don't allow yourself to do that. Listen to me. Everyone goes through these seasons in life; you are not alone or unique in this respect. Everyone you know has been through something. Let the tough times make you a better and wiser person, not a foolish one.

What do you think about on-line dating for Christians?

Personally, I'm not a fan, but there are many who would disagree with me on that. We have couples in our church who met on-line and are happily married today.

However you meet someone, you must give yourself time to get to know the person. Too many singles jump into relationships too quickly. Remember that communication via the internet creates a false sense of intimacy. You begin thinking you really know the other person. Actually, if you have only been communicating on-line, you honestly do not know the individual at all. You have an image in your mind of who the person is, but it takes face to face, real time interaction to know someone. It does not matter how pretty, how fine, or how rich the person is.

You must ask good questions, listen well and watch behavior. Do not get swooned by his strength or her curves or the sweet talk. Where does the person go to church? Ask for the name of the pastor. Find out if the person has been submitted to anyone for the last few years. More than anything, you must be safe. If you go on a date with someone you have met online, go to a public place, make sure you have transportation to get home, and let someone know where you will be. Do not go to the person's house, or bring the individual to your house.

If you are a member of Faith Fellowship, and you think there is some potential, immediately contact one of the pastors and let us interview and get to know the person. If you belong to another church, talk to your pastor or a church elder and remain honest and accountable. Give someone who has your best interests in mind permission to help you remain responsible and sane during the dating process. Please, for your sake, there must be no kissing and no sexual activity. Physical intimacy will lead you to a deeper false sense of thinking that you know this person. Do not let your desire to be with someone override your ability to think clearly.

Children are never mistakes. But how can my child's father make the same mistake three times with three different women and then accuse me of falling into sexual sin for having a relationship with him when I was the first one he had a child with? We are no longer together.

I hear a blame game going on. *Your sin is worse than mine. You sinned just like me.* He is accusing you because he used you. You are accusing him because you are hurt and are now raising a child alone. You did fall into sexual sin, but blaming each other is not going to change what has happened.

The fact of the matter is that you weren't married when you got together and then a baby was born. We thank God for the life of your child. God loves this little one. He has a plan for your child and is going to bless him or her. But for a man to go out and have another baby with another woman that he is not married to and then another baby with another woman after that, well, what can we say? Do you see any progress in this man's life? So why are you surprised that he is finding fault with you?

And now what happens? All of these children walk around with no daddy. They end up hurt individuals looking for someone or something to fill the daddy void. We cannot pretend that children do not need a father, and we must stop acting as if a father's role is unnecessary. Dads are essential in their children's lives. God's intention was and is for a husband and a wife to have children. Sex is not a game.

Get your life together and be the best mom to your child that you can be. You are now a saved, born again believer. You are a woman of God, and God has a future for you and your child. Stop wasting your time getting into foolish arguments over whose sin is worse than the other's. Go forward honoring God and teach your child to do the same.

Is it wrong to like someone in church when you are in a program trying to change your life around?

No, it's not wrong to like someone.

You have to be honest with yourself, though. Are you ready to enter into a relationship knowing that you are in a program that is helping you to heal from past hurts and current hang-ups? Are you prepared for a relationship while you are in a program that is aimed at making you a healthier and wiser you? If, at this point in your life, liking someone is going to throw you back into old habits and thought patterns, then it might be best to wait a while and work on yourself first.

We prefer to short-circuit healing and restoration. We sometimes think, "I got this," and we move too quickly. Allow yourself time. It's not wrong to have affection for somebody, but make sure the time is right to move forward in that area. Talk to your program leaders. They care about you and want what's best for you. Do not walk around with a secret longing. Be accountable. Part of your recovery is learning to build honest and close friendships.

Again, it's not wrong to have a fondness for someone provided you are not 'in lust' and you are not being foolish. That being said, of course it would be wrong if the other person is already married or engaged. I encourage you to quickly find an older Christian of the same sex, someone you trust, and bring him/her along side you as an accountability partner.

Do you believe in soul mates? If so, how would you define a soul mate?

I think you are asking if there are "marriages made in heaven." Can two people come together and know they are absolutely supposed to be together? Yes, absolutely; just like two people can come together and know that they are absolutely not supposed to be together.

When people fall in love, they feel like soul mates. You give your vow to someone at the altar before God, and you know you love each other. However, even if you believe you were made for each other, there will come a time when you don't like your soul brother or sister, and the whole soul thing goes out the window.

There are many cultures where arranged marriages are the norm. They believe that love comes after marriage. What does this tell us? Should we consider whether we put too much emphasis on our feelings? Love is an act of your will. Let me say that again: Love is an act of your will. You learn to grow in love and to act more and more lovingly because of your commitment to love someone. Once you marry, you will find out that the feelings of love and excitement come and go. The reality of this separates the adults from the child-like minded. Staying in love once the lovey-dovey feelings have faded takes active participation, determination, and recognition that *this is the person I married; this is the person I chose. I'm going to work to make it work.* Of course, some couples are more compatible than others. Others learn to be compatible. It all takes time and work.

Is there one person on the earth that you are meant to marry? Some people hold to that belief. Over time, though, you may find that you have strong attractions to another person who is not your mate. Maturity is recognizing that these seemingly overwhelming feelings will either fester and grow or eventually die out, depending on what *you do* with them – whether you feed them or starve them. Let's say you are married and you are struggling in your marriage. You meet someone who really rings your bell. The person is compassionate, open minded, a good listener, and whatever it may be that you believe has the potential to fill the void you feel your mate is causing. Suddenly, you think you have met your soul mate! No, you have not. You are infatuated because a part of you feels unfulfilled. You are attracted, and attraction is not wrong. Acting on that attraction, getting emotionally or physically close to that other person is wrong. You have to go to your mate and work on your marriage. This is honorable to God.

So, when you fall in love, and you know you want to get married, make sure it's the right person and then jump in... and don't jump out. Your mate is your soul mate.

I continuously ask God to bring my fiancé home from jail, but He doesn't? Do you think it is God's plan for us to be together?

Well, I cannot say it is God's plan because I don't know if your fiancé is saved or not. If he is not saved and you are, then it's not God's will or timing for the two of you to be together because God would not desire for you to be yoked together with an unbeliever.

Secondly, I don't know why this man is in jail. If you were my daughter, I would say you probably could rethink this. Why is he in jail? Has he changed since being in there? There is no guarantee that he will change when he gets out. I don't know how long he is going to be in prison or if he is going to be able to provide for you when he gets released.

Maybe God is not letting him out of jail because he really committed a crime and is guilty. The law says if you are guilty of committing a crime, then you must do the time. So God is not bound to your prayers to let him out of jail.

We thank God that He does have grace and mercy. I've told you before that when you are guilty, the last thing you want in court is justice. You want mercy and you want grace. However, God is not bound to release someone from prison if the person has committed a crime.

You are not tied to this man as a mate in marriage. It's possible that your letting go will help him want to help himself.

155

Maybe if you release him from your heart, he will choose to get the help he needs which begins with his turning to the Lord.

I've been living with my boyfriend since October. We have both recently given our lives to God. Now we are feeling guilty because we are not married. What should we do?

First of all, I want to honor you for asking the question and for dealing with your guilt. You are both believers now, and you recognize that God's design is for a man and a woman to be married. You have three options. (Actually, you have four.) Number one: If you cannot contain yourselves sexually, then let us marry you off tomorrow. That is one option, and "that takes care of that" so to speak. It takes care of your current lust issue, but it does not take care of any long-term lust issues. Remember, marriage is not going to make particular problems or concerns go away, so consider carefully if the two of you are truly ready to entrust yourselves to each other for the rest of your lives. Number two: One of you moves out, you both get pre-marital counseling, and then plan your wedding. Number three: If it is not possible or prudent for one of you to move out, and you are truly committed to God, make a pledge to each other that you are not going to be sexually intimate until you get married. Move into different rooms or do whatever you have to do to stay pure. This is not for everyone because not everyone can handle this. For many, the temptation is simply too strong, which is unfortunate because you want to be able to trust each other enough and love each other enough to wait. The fourth option is to break up; however, it sounds like you both wish to be together and want to do what is right in the sight of God.

My boyfriend and I have only prayed together to bless our food, and I have been too shy to ask him to pray with me. I don't want to push him into it, so what do you think I should say?

Say, "Boyfriend, would you like to pray together from time to time?" See what he says. I am interpreting your shyness as fear. What are you afraid he is going to say? What are you afraid he might do? Go ahead and ask him. Tell him that it means a lot to you when you both pray over your food, and then ask if he thinks you could maybe pray together more regularly. That will give you a good temperature of where his heart and mind are.

I do wonder, however, about your inability to be honest in this relationship. If you are fearful of asking simple questions, are you going to be able to openly share your heart with this person? Are you in a relationship in which you are afraid to be yourself? Is that what you want for your life? Do him the favor of allowing him to get to know the woman you really are. Do yourself a favor and find out what you are afraid of and why. Give yourself an opportunity to mature in this area. Be honest with him and with yourself.

We know that marriage is ordained by God and is something that most singles aspire to. Considering that not all single people will marry, what encouragement would you offer to the unmarried?

If you can be content living single – stay single. If you cannot, there is nothing wrong with wanting to be married. For this season during which you are single (and we don't know how long it will be), enjoy your life! Serve God, serve in a ministry, and go have fun. Find a profession that you feel passionate about. Work as unto the Lord and, again, go have fun. Take trips, spend time with friends, and keep your life pure from sin. You will see that you don't need a man or woman in your life in order to feel content or happy. No, you won't be involved in sexual activity, but sexual activity does not define a full life. Your life will be very full because you are not sitting at home in front of the television night after night longing for what you do not have and wishing your life was different.

My encouragement to the unmarried is to live!

Too many people believe that marriage will make them happy. Marriage does not make you happy. God and you make you happy. Stop focusing on what you do not have and deal with what life has to offer right now. Above all, do not isolate yourself.

Make sure you are part of a small group such as a home group or a prayer group. You want to be in an accountability group of some kind that meets regularly and where you are building close relationships. You need other people in your world. As you enjoy your life, establish solid connections with other believers who will walk with you through good times and bad. Being single does not mean you have to be all alone all the time. Develop sincere friendships and have the benefit of a full life.

How do you know if someone is right for you?

If you are paying attention, you will definitely know when someone is **not** right for you! And when you know someone is not right for you, you must let that person go. Sometimes we want to be with someone so badly that we compromise in areas we know we should not. We sometimes compromise to our own detriment.

Introduce him/her to your family and your close friends. What do they say about the person? Visit the person's home church and meet the pastor. What does the pastor think about him or her? Meet his or her friends. What kind of people are they? Pay attention to reactions and moods. How does this person handle situations when irritated, angry, or frustrated? You want to observe your new interest in many situations.

You have to be sure that you are in love with the actual person and not the idealized person you have mentally created. Are you in love with an image in your mind which blinds you to the reality of who the person is? Do the person's words and actions line up? Is this really a good catch, or are you fooling yourself?

Whatever you do, do not begin running around saying, "God brought me this person." Wait and get to know the person before you decide that he or she is God's gift to you. Your perception of being in love may just be your hormones talking or your loneliness screaming or a familiar dysfunctional attraction playing on your brain. Getting to know someone takes time. You don't want to rush in and later wish you had waited just a little longer to be sure.

Paul says that unmarried people should remain unmarried. Please explain.

He means that if you are unmarried, stay unmarried. However, remember, context is everything. Paul is speaking to the believers in Corinth, and he is talking about Christian men and women who divorce without biblical grounds. He says that, according to the Word of the Lord, they cannot remarry unless the divorce was because of adultery. He says they should either remain unmarried or reconcile their marriage. This is hard for many people to hear, and it's really a binding kind of text even though we don't practice it enough in Christianity. We know that God is a God of grace, and He is a God of second chances. The restriction is not meant to put a guilt trip on anyone; however, you know God's theology on marriage: one man wedded to one woman all the days of their lives until death.

It is a sobering text, which is all the more reason to choose your mate very wisely. Someone told me once that you cannot help who you fall in love with. Really? Think about it. You choose to love or not to love. If you become attracted to someone and he or she is already married, you have to make a decision to stay away from that person. If you don't, inappropriate feelings will develop. If you are attracted to an unbeliever or someone who is not headed in the same direction as you are in life, you must guard your heart, or you will end up giving it away to the wrong person. Paul states, and I believe all of us who are married would agree, that if you are unmarried, you have options and opportunities that married folks cannot consider because they have to consider each other, their children, etc. Some people are fine in an unmarried state. Others have much difficulty with it. If you are a discontented single, just know that marriage will bring its own challenges.

I am a twenty-eight year old, single woman. By the grace of God, I have managed to remain pure. I am doing my best to take advantage of my singleness by becoming God's best while waiting, but sometimes the desire for marriage, a husband, and a family becomes overwhelming. Is it possible to have a strong desire for a husband and it not be God's will for my life? Is it possible that maybe God does not desire for me to be married?

One of the ways you know that you have the gift of singleness is that the desire to be married is not overwhelming all the time. In other words, you are not constantly consumed with the desire for a mate. The feelings may come, but you are able to get through those overwhelming moments – meaning they come for maybe a day or two, or a week or so, and then they pass and you are okay again. Some people can handle those overwhelming zones and are fine. These people have the gift of singleness. It does not necessarily mean they will remain single forever, but they are content in their singleness and could be single for the rest of their lives and be perfectly fine with it.

But if being single is really a challenge for you and is overwhelming, then it's likely that God is not calling you to be single. So begin to ask Him for a mate, and ask your close friends to join you in this prayer.

Scripture says you'll be happier if you are single, unless you just simply cannot handle being single. Here is what the Bible says to the married couples: If you get married, you will have trouble. I'll let you in on a secret. I thought I could disprove that idea because I am the easiest guy in the world to get along with. When I got married, I thought it would be a piece of cake for my wife because I am so easy going. Turns out, I'm easy to get along with *for me* because I see myself through my own eyes. My wife will tell you differently. Marriage is not an easy road to travel.

I encourage you, in your desire to be married, to continue to grow into the woman that God would have you be. Continue to take care of yourself and do those things that will make you the kind of woman you would want your son to marry. Talk to your mature Christian friends and let them know that you would like to meet someone. Get out and get around people often.

You are not wrong for wanting to be married. Just be careful not to let the desire become the main focus of your life. Sometimes we focus so much on a desire, we stop living a fruitful life. Don't focus on what you lack; live your life to the fullest right now. Continue to be thankful for what you do have. God knows your heart's desire, and He is faithful.

I'd like to offer a prayer for our singles right now: *Lord, in Jesus' name, I pray for the singles who desire to walk in Your perfect will. I pray for this young sister and for all those like her who want to honor You in their singleness but are sometimes overwhelmed by desires for marriage and companionship. Lord, I ask that You embrace them and make Your perfect will for their* lives abundantly clear. God, give them the strength to stand against every temptation and every lie of the enemy. In Jesus' name we pray, Amen.

I have been in a three and a half year relationship. We want to get married but don't have the money for it right now. Would eloping to Reno or Vegas be a bad thing?

No, eloping would not be a bad thing, but we can do it right here for you for free. We have married hundreds of couples in our offices, and it doesn't cost you a thing. I hope you are not sleeping together. If you are living together, then one of you should find the floor or the couch or a spare bedroom to sleep in until we can marry you off.

Can I still be saved if I am living with my boyfriend, and we have a baby together?

A person is saved when he or she accepts Jesus Christ as his or her Lord (this means Master – He speaks, and you do what he commands) and Savior. At that point, there is repentance and a commitment to turning away from sin.

The sin is not that you are a heterosexual female living in the same dwelling with a man. The sin is that you are having sexual relations with a man who is not your husband. If you are intimately involved with him, you must stop because you are a Christian.

You may think to yourself, "He might leave me." Well, you will have to choose between God and your boyfriend. You have to make up your mind that you are going to serve the Lord. Hopefully, this man won't be so foolish as to turn away from a beautiful woman like yourself or from his child. If he loves you so much that he has begun a family with you, then the two of you need to get some counseling and get married.

As a Christian, you have to take a stand and respect the Lord. So, if you are genuinely saved, you will try to stop this sin immediately. Ask the Lord to help you do that which honors Him. You want to let your light shine and live out an example of a godly woman before this man. Do what you know is right according to the Word of God. Also, continue to pray for your man's salvation.

CHAPTER 13

Prayer

I am going through a rough period in my life right now. I have kept my faith, but I still feel depressed. What prayer can you give me to start my day off to keep me grounded?

I would direct anyone, especially if you are going through a hard time, to always pray the Word of God. In prayer, remind yourself of what the Word says. Try beginning with Philippians 4:4 which says, "Rejoice in the Lord always, and again I say, rejoice." The passage then moves you right into the following words: "Be anxious for nothing," and that *nothing* in Greek means *absolutely, positively not one thing.* Be anxious for not one thing. It goes on and reminds you how to think. Think on things that are true, noble, just, pure, lovely, things that are of good report, and things that are virtuous and praiseworthy. It reminds you to keep your mind focused on what is in the Word.

Personalize it. "I am anxious for nothing, not even one thing, but I am lifting all cares up to You, Lord. I give You my petitions with thanksgiving. I thank You. I offer You thanks for who You are and for what You are doing in my life..." Personalize that passage every single day. "I rejoice in the Lord always, and again I say to myself, 'Rejoice.'" Begin there and go through to the end, every day, praying for yourself. This start will help get you into the habit of praying through the Scriptures.

Praying the Word of God encourages your spirit and redirects your thinking to what God says. With practice, you will begin to elevate His Word above the anxious thoughts within you. Go to the Psalms and pray the Psalms. The words are there for you. Personalize them. For example, if you are reading Psalm 34, remind yourself: "I will bless the Lord at all times. His praise will continually be in my mouth. My soul will make its boast in the Lord... God, I am going to give You praise. I am always going to give You praise. No matter what I am going through, I am going to offer praise to You." You will begin to see a difference as you reflect on God's love and nature as revealed in the Scriptures.

If your depression is clinical, you also need to seek medical assistance to find out what can be done to help balance out your brain chemicals and your emotions. However, if you are struggling because you are in a difficult season, begin to pray and meditate on the truth of God's Word. Your thinking and outlook will gradually shift as you make His truth the main focus of your daily life.   It is also okay to talk to a pastor, a Christian counselor, or a godly friend. Reach out to someone who will give you the truth with love.

How do you anoint someone's house?

Sometimes the pastors and I go to someone's house, and we take anointing oil and anoint over the doorposts and throughout the home. We pray God's peace in and over the dwelling. It is not magic or superstition. We are asking God to bless the home and cover it with His peace, love, and protection.

God spoke to people in the Bible. He speaks to people now. He has never spoken to me, even when I ask Him. Why?

God does speak to us. The most important way God speaks is through the Scriptures, so read your Bible. Another way He speaks is through His Spirit. As you mature in the Lord, you will get a sense of the voice of the Holy Spirit. I have walked with God for thirty-plus years now. I have never heard the audible voice of God, but in my spirit I know the voice of the Holy Spirit.

The Old Testament book of 1 Samuel tells the story of a young boy named Samuel.

One night, while Samuel was lying down, the Lord called to him. Samuel thought the priest Eli was calling him. He ran to Eli and said, "Here I am; you called me."

Eli said, "I didn't call you; go back and lie down."

Samuel went back. He heard someone call his name again, "Samuel!" So he ran back to Eli thinking the priest was summoning him.

"Here I am; you called me," he said again.

Eli responded, "I didn't call you; go back and lie down."

Samuel went back and heard the voice a third time, "Samuel!"

He ran back to Eli again. "I didn't call you," Eli said. Eli realized that the Lord was calling Samuel, so he told the boy, "If he calls you, say, 'Speak, Lord, for your servant is listening.'"

Samuel then realized, "Okay, now I know the voice of the Lord." The next time he heard his name called, he responded, "Speak, Lord, your servant is listening," and the Lord spoke to him (1 Samuel 3). This was an audible voice, but I do not personally know anyone who has heard God's audible voice. The takeaway from this story is to be open to the Lord and to His speaking into your life.

God may choose to speak through circumstances. Circumstances can sometimes be an indication of God revealing something to you or leading you in a certain direction. The Lord also speaks by giving a sense of His peace. Do you have peace on the inside, or do you feel turmoil about something? You'll learn to discern whether the turmoil is simply fear of moving forward, or if it's an "unsettling" sense you have indicating that this is not the right decision.

We have the Word of God, the Spirit of God, circumstances, and a sense of peace. Remember, God also uses other people in our lives such as our pastors, our spouse, and close friends. When unsure, get sound counsel and wise advice from mature believers who know you and love Jesus.

Is it okay to pray in Yahweh's name?

The Bible says to pray in the name of the Lord Jesus Christ. Because we love and trust in Jesus and have put our faith in him, we are able to go directly to the Father in prayer. In John 16:23, Jesus says "...my Father will give you whatever you ask in my name." Pray to the Father in the name of the Lord Jesus Christ.

Jesus taught us to love and pray for people. How do we pray for those who deny Jesus and his gift of unconditional love and forgiveness when they refuse to accept it?

Those are the exact people you pray for – the people who are denying God's love and won't accept His Son, Jesus Christ. Initially, Paul the Apostle blatantly denied and rejected this love. He wouldn't accept it. According to Romans 16, he had relatives who were in Christ before he was. We can pretty much guarantee that those relatives were praying for Paul. By the way, Paul's condition got worse before it got better. He became an increasingly violent and destructive man. At the end of that road, however, was salvation!

Pray for those who are denying God's gift of salvation because that is just their present state. How many of you remember when you were denying God's love and didn't want to believe in Jesus? There was a time when we all were there.

Continue praying for those who reject God's love. Continue displaying a godly, Christ-like character to them. Be genuine in love and concern for them.

How do we really get closer to God?
The Bible says, "Draw near to God, and He will draw near to you" (James 4:8). Think about a human relationship for a moment. If you wanted to get closer to the person you love, your spouse or

your fiancé, what would you do? You would spend time with the person. You would talk in an endearing manner. You would make room in your life for the person you care about, and you would sacrifice for him or her. It's no different with the Lord. The Lord says that as much as you want to get close to Him, He is even more willing to get close to you.

Reading the Word, praying, spending time in worship, cultivating an attitude of thankfulness, spending time in fellowship with other believers, and serving others all help develop a closer relationship with the Lord. There isn't a list of rules or regulations to follow in order to get closer to God. Submit yourself to Him – you decrease and let Him increase in your life.

Where in the Bible does it say to pray for those in authority? I only see where it says to submit to authority. If Jesus prayed for authority, what were the results?

Take a look at 1 Timothy 2:1-4. Scripture exhorts us to put up petitions, requests, and prayers for those who are in authority such as kings and leaders over a nation, that we might live peaceful and quiet lives in godliness and reverence.

We must pray for our government officials.

Jesus offered himself up for all people. He took on the sins of all of us – this includes your sins, my sins, our leaders' sins, etc. Our leaders carry a lot of responsibility. We pray that God would grant them wisdom and discernment to lead our nation in righteousness. We pray for their protection, for their families, and for the many decisions they must make. We ask God to guide and lead them as they lead us. We ask that their hearts and minds would be turned to the things of God, and that they would honor Him in their decision making.

We don't have a king to pray for, but we have a president, and we have elected and appointed government, city, and state leaders. We also have bosses and supervisors. We are to pray for those in authority.

I have been praying for the removal of a situation at work for two years. I am being placed closer to the person I want to be removed from. How should I change my prayer to be more effective?

You always have to consider situations through a God lens. Maybe God is trying to teach you something by putting you closer to the person. Ask Him what He wants you to learn in this situation. You've asked for removal, but He has not granted that just yet. If anything, you are experiencing the very opposite of your prayer – so you must begin to look for the lesson in the trial.

Are you praising Him even though the situation is not to your liking? Are you thanking Him for all of His blessings, or have you begun to focus most of your mental energy and attention on how much you hate working with the person in question and on the situation you want changed?

The Bible says we do not know how to pray as we ought to, but the Holy Spirit intercedes for us according to the mind of God (Romans 8:26-27). You can ask the Holy Spirit to intercede for you in this situation. Jesus ever lives to make intercession for you. Take a look at Hebrews 7:25 and Romans 8:28-37, and let these verses be an encouragement to you.

Continue to ask God what He is trying to show you because maybe the Lord is going to use you. Maybe he is going to use your godliness to affect that person. Read Luke 6:27–38. It is a challenging passage that talks about loving our enemies. The very idea of doing good to those who mistreat us goes against the fiber of our natural being, but all of us are learning to walk according to the Spirit of God and not according to the flesh. If you are being challenged in this way, it could be an indication that this is the time and season for you to mature in this area of your spiritual walk.

What has this person done that you dislike him or her so much? Have you been praying for the individual? Begin to pray for the person and ask the Lord to use you according to His will, not according to how you feel.

***I study the Bible and I pray. To be honest, I really don't know
how to pray for what I want. I don't know what to say when I'm
praying. I've had so many requests and problems in my life.
How can I pray in a way that God will hear me?***

If you are praying in faith and in the name of Jesus Christ, you are
being heard. Try not to be anxious or nervous when you begin to
pray. God hears you. It's not a matter of saying the right words or
using the right prayer formula. The Lord is not only your heavenly
Father, His Spirit is your Counselor and close Friend. Just talk to
Him. As you read and study the Scriptures, you will gain deeper
understanding of who God is and how much He loves you. The
more you know about Him, the more you will grow to love and trust
Him, and you will become more comfortable talking to Him.

We all need to grow and develop. I would recommend
you find a mature Christian of the same sex, sit down together, and
let that person talk to you. We all need a mentor in our lives,
somebody who is beyond where we are to show us things we
currently don't see. All that you "see" is not all there is to see. All
that you know is not all there is to know. God places mature,
experienced brothers and sisters in our lives to help direct, lead,
and guide us. You have to reach out and ask someone to be a
mentor to you. Also, find Scriptures that apply to your situation
and begin to speak and pray them into your life.

Pastor, do we pray differently for those who are unsaved than how we pray for those who are saved?

Yes, in some aspects we do. We pray the unsaved will get saved. We pray their minds and hearts will be open to God's Word and to His love and that the Gospel message will reach them in a manner that is clear and understandable. We pray that the Spirit of God will draw them, that faith would be provided, and that by God's grace they would receive the message and accept the Savior. We also pray for other areas of their lives such as for blessings and for their health and their kids, their marriages, and so on.

I am an older single woman. I am retired and live on a fixed monthly income from Social Security. I do give my ten percent faithfully, and I also I give to the radio and TV broadcasts. I often give a little extra to various ministries, just because. When we pray for the offering and for the financial needs of the congregation, I simply bow my head and agree. However, I do not get any more than my Social Security, so how do or how would the prayers possibly come to pass for me financially?

Wow, I appreciate your faithfulness, and God sees your faithfulness. His Word says that the righteous will not be forsaken, nor their seed begging bread (Psalm 37:25). Your basic needs are being met by way of our Social Security system here in America, and you are thankful for that. Let's ask the Lord to move on your behalf.

I would like to take a moment and call on the Lord right now – *God, in the Name of Jesus, we ask that You show our sister, in her faithfulness, the above and beyond the income she is receiving from Social Security. Father, she continues to be faithful. She continues to bless Your body and the work of Your church. Lord, we ask You to open the windows of heaven and bless her financially, so she can say, "Now, that is GOD in my life!" We ask that You would surprise her by Your goodness and perform a financial miracle in her life.*

God can do it. Don't you doubt it.

I have a condition that affects my ability to focus and am very easily distracted. When I try to pray, I often lose my concentration, and it is hard for me to stay focused for long stretches of time. Do you think my prayers will not avail much because they are not long?

Think for a moment. Do you think God knows about your condition? It is not your fault that you have this condition. God is not blaming you for anything. God never said, "Let your prayers be long that I might hear them." In fact, Jesus said we should not keep babbling when we pray. We pray in faith and ask God regarding our needs (Matthew 6:5-7).

If you are reading this, and you can relate to what this person is saying, here is what I want you to do. Put your hand on your head right now and declare, "In the Name of Jesus Christ, I have the mind of Christ, and my mind is being transformed and renewed. I shall begin to concentrate on things that are worth my time. I will be a strong and able thinker, and I will be dedicated in prayer. Amen."

Nowhere does the Bible say that a prayer has to be long to be heard. We are instructed to pray in faith and to pray continually. God hears you.

CHAPTER 14

Tithing

I have a choice between paying my utility bills and paying my tithes. I plan on paying my tithes first, but that will leave my utility bill unpaid. What do I do?

In all honesty, if you pay your tithe and don't pay the world system, then the world system can talk against Christians. Go ahead and pay your utility bill. However, listen closely; come in and let us sit down with you and help you with your finances. Most likely, you are not handling your finances correctly. It's possible you are not living on a budget. You may be spending God's money in other places and then are trying to feel holy by paying your tithes and not paying your bills. You need to get your entire budget in order. We need to work out a plan where you pay your tithes *and* pay your bills as well. There is more to biblical financial blessing than just tithing, and you must learn and apply all of the principles.

I have been giving tithes and offerings for thirty years. I watch my spending and try to buy what I really need, but I struggle with poverty. What am I doing wrong?

When you say you are struggling with poverty, is that a poverty mentality? You need to sit down with someone and talk together about how you go about life. What is your education, and what is your job capability as far as career and salary? How high can you go up the professional or vocational ladder? Are there any entrepreneurial ideas that you can come up with, or can we help get you out of your current job and into a better one? How much are you spending on housing? Where are you spending your money, and what are you spending it on? All of these questions would have to be asked and considered. Do not accept a poverty attitude. Do not accept it.

Believe that God wants to bless you. Stand on His promises and then do your part. In His Word He has given us practical ideas which are principles of financial stability. It sounds like you need financial guidance.

What advice can you give me? I want to tithe but am on a very tight budget. I am worried that if I pay my tithes, I won't have enough for other things.

You say you cannot afford to give to God. I say you can't afford *not* to give to God. The last thing you want is God out of your finances. We could ask people right now to stand up and testify about how God has shown Himself faithful in their lives as they have been obedient in putting Him first in regard to their finances. Do you need some help with your budget?

Handling money takes knowledge and discipline. We must learn to live within our income by disciplining ourselves to do so. Please see my book *Be A Man* in which we discuss the importance of your honoring God by living a financially disciplined life. We also have a three-CD teaching on building your faith in regard to your finances.

Scripture does not say you will have everything you want; however, you will have everything you need. There may be times of blessing and prosperity in your life, but the Lord will allow you to go through times of financial tightness as well. Philippians 4:11 is a reminder that God wants you to learn to be content in every situation. The verse closely following that one says, "...for I can do all things through Christ who strengthens me" (Philippians 4:13). These words are being spoken in a financial context. We learn to be content in times of bounty and in difficult financial times as well.

Be faithful to the Lord. It is God's promise to take care of you – and He keeps His Word.

My wife and I have different thoughts on tithing. She says we should give ten percent of the gross; I say we should give ten percent of the net. Who is right?

This is really a faith issue. Wherever you are with your faith, let it be that. Whatever the husband eventually says, the wife is called to come into agreement with him on the matter. You are not being unbiblical; however, your faith may be a bit smaller than hers in this area. Keep in mind that tithing on the net means that when you get a tax return, you then tithe on that too. If you tithe on the gross, you don't have to tithe on the tax return because you already tithed on that money. Of course, you still can if you want to. Remember, you can't out-give God!

Try tithing on the gross for a season (maybe three months) and see what happens. Or, if you are a two income household, you tithe on the net and your wife can tithe on the gross. Whatever you decide, do not argue over it.

When Abraham returned from the war, how did he know that he had to give a tithe to the King of Salem, the priest Melchizedek?

The answer establishes for us that tithing is not under the law, for Abraham lived four hundred and thirty years before the law was given. Tithing was a means of honoring and worshiping God.

Remember, there were no people serving God except Abraham at that time. Melchizedek is referred to as "priest of God Most High." Abraham saw him as representative of God and gave him a tenth as a form of worship unto the Lord (Genesis 14:18-20, Hebrews 7:1-2). (We believe Melchizedek is a pre-figuration of Christ because he had no beginning of days, no end of life, no genealogy, and he disappeared.)

Even Abraham's grandson Jacob tithed. Jacob's story is a bit different (Genesis 28). When Jacob realized that God wanted to bless him, he said to God, "If You go with me and protect me and bless me, I will give you a tenth of everything I acquire." He was stating, "You are my God. You are responsible for all I have. I give back to you what is already Yours."

Tithing predates the law, and tithing exists after the law. In Matthew 23:23, Jesus told the religious leaders and the teachers of the law that they were tithing the littlest herbs in their houses but had forgotten about justice and mercy and faith. He told them they should have practiced the latter without neglecting the former (tithing).

I haven't been able to give my tithes because of my finances. I give what I can when I can. Does God still love me just the same?

Yes, God loves you even if you don't tithe. You can't change His love; it's unconditional. In your heart, though, you seem to know that you should be tithing. If you did not believe that, you would not be asking the question. I would like to challenge your ability to handle money and live within a budget. It sounds like you need financial counseling. We often don't know how to handle money, and we spend much more than we make. We rob God to pay off other things and, as a result, we pull away from Him. I encourage you to take a look at Philippians 4:12. If you are living beyond your income, some adjustments must be made both financially and mentally. Get financial counseling and learn to balance your budget, then maybe you will be willing and able to tithe.

Are we supposed to tithe on gifts of money as well as our income?

Technically, we are not required to tithe on a gift, but we are to give ten percent of our income. That being said, can we tithe on gifts? Absolutely. If we tithe on everything, we still cannot out-give God. People who are really blessed have often increased their giving beyond the tithe. Many go from giving ten percent to giving even more. Some folks go to fifteen percent, then from fifteen percent to twenty percent because they have learned that the best investment is not in Wall Street or in stocks and bonds. The very best investment is in trusting God, and God always gives back.

I am a single parent with three kids, and I work two part time jobs. I put money in the basket on Sundays, as much as I can. But sometimes it comes down to buying food or tithing. Is this okay?

Yes. Would you please call and make an appointment with us (or with your pastors) and get some help in creating a budget? It is especially when we are in those tight financial situations that we have to depend on God. We will show you how to establish and build faith by creating a sound financial plan and managing your money in such a way that your giving is a part of this budget. We definitely want you to take care of your needs, and we want you to take care of your family. God wants you to have wisdom. As you grow in faith, you will see that God will bless you as you tithe and give. You don't want to take God's money and spend it somewhere else, so we will help you.

CHAPTER 15

Mormons and Jehovah's Witnesses

Are Mormons considered saved when they believe God and Jesus are separate people?

Mormon theology states that Jesus and Lucifer were blood brothers. Many Mormons don't know this, and it offends many of them when they hear it. Their theology also says, "As God is, man shall become; as man is, God once was." Think about that for a moment. Think about the implications of that statement.

Paul warned, "But I am afraid that just as Eve was deceived by the serpent's cunning, your minds may somehow be led astray from your sincere and pure devotion to Christ. For if someone comes to you and preaches a Jesus other than the Jesus we preached, or if you receive a different spirit from the Spirit you received or a different gospel from the one you accepted, you put up with it easily enough" (2 Corinthians 11:3-4).

This kind of deception is what we believe has happened to Mormons. It is clear from Mormon theology that their views are not biblical. The Jesus they are preaching is not the Jesus from the Bible. Sadly, their younger converts often don't understand this reality. Their Jesus is a Jesus from the earlier writings of Joseph Smith: *The Doctrines of Covenants, The Pearl of Great Price,* and *The Book of Mormon.*

The Scriptures make it abundantly clear that false teachers would arise and preach another gospel to deceive people (see Galatians 1:6-9).

How can I talk to Mormons who want to discuss theology?

That would depend on how well you know your Bible. If you feel fairly confident in your knowledge of Scripture, then engage freely. However, there are some teachings in the Mormon faith that even some Mormons are not aware of. For example, many Mormons are not told about the original doctrines of their founders Joseph Smith and Brigham Young. These men believed that Jesus and Lucifer (Satan) were brothers. They also believed that Adam resurrected and had intercourse with Mary, and that is how Jesus was conceived. Another very troubling theology of the Mormon faith is "As man is, God once was, and as God is, man shall become." These very disturbing beliefs cause a huge doctrinal chasm between the Mormon Church and Orthodox Christianity.

Such beliefs change the very nature of Christ and the message of salvation. As Paul said in 2 Corinthians 11:3-4, people preach a different Jesus than what has been preached.

Mormonism was begun by Joseph Smith by way of a supposed visitation from an angel named Moroni who Smith says gave him the "true" faith. However, some eighteen hundred years earlier, Paul had said in Galatians 1:6-9, "...if we or an angel from heaven should preach to you a gospel other than the one we preached to you, let them be accursed by God." It is interesting that the Prophet Mohammed (the founder of Islam) also said he was visited by an angel who gave him all the information for the Koran.

Thank God that the Scriptures had already warned us that these inconsistent and false ideas would appear. Joseph Smith received his supposed angelic visitation in about 1830 A.D. and

Muhammad around 600 A.D., both long after Paul had written his letter to the Galatians.

To effectively talk theology with those spouting a different Jesus, learn your Bible. Know who Christ is according to the Word of God.

How are we different from Jehovah's Witnesses? What scriptures would you suggest I lean on when in conversation with them?

Jehovah's Witnesses do read and know their Bibles fairly well. They are taught and trained how to argue against born again Christians. The main differences are our belief in the Trinity, the person of Jesus being God the Son and equal with the Father in essence, and the way of salvation. There are many other differences, but I will limit my answer to these for now.

Concerning the Trinity, the term "Trinity" is not found in the Bible. It is a term coined to describe the unity of the Godhead – God the Father, God the Son, and God the Holy Spirit. Because the Bible says there is but one God, yet identifies all three persons as God in perfect harmony and unity, this union came to be called the "Tri-Unity" of God, or the shortened version, "Trinity." We hold this view because, although the word Trinity is not in the Bible, the Tri-Unity of God is clearly expressed in Scripture and is biblical.

We know the Bible calls the Father, God (John 17:1-5; John 6:45-46, Romans 1:1-7, and many other passages). We know the Bible identifies Jesus the Son as God (John 1:1-3; Colossians 1:15-19; Colossians 2:9; Hebrews 1, and many other passages). The Bible also calls the Holy Spirit God, and He is identified as a Person (Acts 5:1-5; Ephesians 4:30; Romans 8:26-27, and other passages), not as a force which is what the Jehovah's Witnesses teach.

Regarding Christ, Jehovah's Witnesses believe Jesus to be a created being and inferior to God. As the referenced verses above state, we know this to be false. Christ is eternal and is one with the Father and the Spirit.

Concerning the way of salvation, the Bible unequivocally teaches that we are saved by grace through faith and not by ANY works on our part (Ephesians 2:8-9), but by belief that God raised Jesus from the dead and by the confession that Jesus is Lord (Romans 10:9-10). We understand that good works or deeds are the *result* of salvation, not the *means* of salvation as the Jehovah's Witnesses believe.

That will get you started. There are good books on the subject which can help you further. One is *Reasoning from the Scriptures with the Jehovah's Witnesses* by Ron Rhodes.

Where do Jehovah's Witnesses get the number 144,000?

The number comes from the Book of Revelation, Chapter 7. Christians believe it refers to the Jews or believers who remain faithful during the Great Tribulation.

For Jehovah's Witnesses, the 144,000 in the Book of Revelation refers to 144,000 leaders who are specially chosen by God. They believe this select group receives salvation and will reign with Jesus when they die. The rest of the Witnesses must work very hard to earn salvation. Remember, Jehovah's Witnesses maintain that there is no hell. So, regarding salvation and eternity, when the 144,000 die, they go to heaven. Other Jehovah's Witnesses will eventually live forever on a new earth, but the souls of the wicked will be destroyed (annihilated). These beliefs are not biblically sound and veer tremendously from Orthodox Christianity.

CHAPTER 16

Understanding Our Faith

What is the difference between a Christian and a born again Christian?

There really is only one kind of Christian, and that is a born again Christian. A born again Christian is someone who has been born from above and has the Spirit of God dwelling within him or her. At some point in time, the person accepted Jesus Christ as Lord and Savior and made a decision to follow him.

There are many so-called Christians who are not really born again. Anybody can say, "I'm a Christian," and wear the

Christian label.   Maybe the person was born into a family that went to church every week or only on Easter and Mother's Day. Up until about fifteen or twenty years ago, if you were an American, you were pretty much considered a Christian. It was a standard label.

But that's not the Bible's definition of a "Christ-ian." The Bible's definition of a Christian is this: You've confessed that Jesus is Lord, and you are a follower of the Lord Jesus Christ. You believe that he is the Son of God, lived a sinless life, and was crucified for your sins. You believe God raised Jesus from the dead, and Christ is Lord of all. You've made a commitment to Jesus Christ, and you have surrendered your life to him. His Spirit has been given to you and dwells within you. That is a born again Christian.

When you are not well versed in the Bible, how do you speak up about your faith to others when they do not want to believe in the true and living God?

Let me share with you something that happened to me many years ago. I had been saved about four months and was all on fire for God. I loved the Lord and was just getting to know the Bible. A Jehovah's Witness approached me. He was a well-trained, thirty-year believer in the Jehovah's Witness doctrine. He began conversing with me, and that man twisted and turned me every way

196

but loose. By the time he left, I was mad at God for allowing me to get into such a predicament. About an hour later I came to my senses. God used that humiliation as a learning opportunity, and I made a commitment to myself that such a thing would never happen to me again. I promised myself that I would learn the Word the best I could, and so I just began to exhaustingly read and study the Bible. I began to read apologetics. Apologetics is the defense of our faith. I got my hands on any tape of accurate Bible teaching I could find; there were no CD's or downloadable sermons back then! The next time Jehovah's Witnesses came and tried to talk to me, they very much wished they hadn't.

First, get versed in the Word of God. Read it as much as possible, pick up CD's, and download sermons. Whenever you can, read, listen, and learn.

When it comes to sharing Christ, just lovingly share. Share what God has done for you. People are skeptical. They want to know what He has done for you and why they should consider following Him too.

When you are in a conversation with someone who purports to know the Bible, keep bringing them to the truth with a question: Who do you say Jesus is? Make them answer that question. Who is Jesus? Some people say they believe in Jesus, but they do not necessarily believe in the Jesus of the Bible. It is important for us as believers to know and understand what we believe and why. Jesus Christ is the Son of God. He is the center of our faith.

Can you know the difference between folks who simply acknowledge the Savior and those who are truly saved?

Yes, you can. Jesus said, "You shall know them by their fruit" (Matthew 7:20). Just hang around them for a month or two. How do they talk? What do they talk about? What are their interests? Are they hungry for God? Are they hungry for the Word? Do they pray? What is their life like? You can tell. Even though we all may be at different levels of maturity in our Christian walk with God, there has to be some fruit or proof that a person is genuinely born again.

When do you know if you are ready to be water baptized?

If a person believes in his heart that Jesus Christ rose from the dead, and if the person has accepted Christ as Savior, then that person is ready to be water baptized. When a person says, "I'm saved; I'm just not ready to be water baptized," the individual really doesn't know what he or she is saying. When you give your life to Christ and are sincere, you are saved. If you are saved, you need to be water baptized.

We have an extensive teaching on this topic, and we invite you to get a copy. If you would like to find out more, please go to our website at *www.faith-fellowship.us* and check out our Resources Catalog.

Are you saved by your profession of faith in Jesus or when you are baptized?

You are saved by grace through faith in Christ alone. Water baptism is an outward sign of an inward work that has already taken place. Jesus commanded everyone who believes in him to be water baptized. Notice the order – first believe, then get baptized. You are saved by your faith in Christ.

How can I give one hundred percent of myself to Jesus when I don't know one hundred percent of myself? I want to be fully devoted to him.

Give him everything you possibly can. He will figure out the percentage.

Give your whole heart completely to God. What does that mean, and how does that look? It means that you are making a declaration, *As for me and my house, we will serve the Lord* (Joshua 24:15), and you really mean it. You are not simply giving lip service to the words, and you are not simply doing right when or

199

because others are looking. You are putting your words into action and are truly living your faith. You are continuously moving toward God. Does that mean that you are going to be perfect? Of course not. What it does mean, though, is when you sin, when you fall short of the mark, you fall toward the cross and not away from it. Yes, you will make mistakes, but make a commitment to the Lord that you are going to do your best to live for Him and represent Him.

The Word says that He who has begun a good work in you will carry it on to completion (Philippians 1:6). The Holy Spirit is working in you. He directs you and will guide and grant you not only the "want to" of pleasing Him but also the "how to" of walking in His good pleasure (see Philippians 2:13).

God is amazing. How can I give Him more glory than I am giving Him? I want to give Him back everything He has given me and more. How can I compare to that kind of love?

You cannot give God back everything He has given you. He has forgiven your sins. He has accepted you as you are. He sent His Son to die on your behalf that you might have eternal life. How can you possibly give back to make up for all of that? You cannot. What you can do is, as Paul says: Make your life a "living sacrifice, holy and pleasing unto the Lord, which is your spiritual act of worship." The things we do when we are in church, such as singing songs, clapping, lifting our hands, saying *Amen,* and listening to the teaching of the Word are all forms of worship. However, Paul says real worship is giving your entire life over to the Lord Jesus Christ (see Romans 12:1-2).

I'm not sure how to answer when someone asks me how long I have been saved. Should I consider my number of years saved beginning from the time I accepted Jesus or from when I learned what it means to live as a Christian?

If you genuinely accepted Jesus, even though you did not fully understand everything about Christianity, then that was the day you were genuinely born again. Think about a newborn baby. When a child is born, he does not have full understanding and doesn't know very much, but he's still a bona fide human being. He's alive. The day you gave your heart to Christ was the beginning of your Christianity. From there you began to grow and learn.

Sometimes people make an emotional decision for Christ, and it's not really a heart decision – it's not a commitment. They're jut saying the words in a moment of emotion. Maybe they hear a message that is inspirational, exciting, or tender. Perhaps the worship is particularly moving, and the Spirit of God is present. Unbelievers can sense that something is *different*, and they think, *I believe in God now. I'm a believer!* In reality, they have had an emotional reaction to an experience, but there is no repentant heart in accepting Jesus Christ by faith. In accepting Christ, we recognize our wretchedness. We realize we are sinful human beings. We understand that we need him to save us, and without him we are lost.

I am not so sure how important counting the years or days is in the long run. Are you serving Christ now? Are you living for him? Are you maturing in your faith, or are you the same carnal (angry, spiteful, bitter, unforgiving, greedy, lustful... you fill in the adjective) person you were before you met Christ? When do you believe you were truly born again? Many people will say something like, "I accepted Christ when I was a child, but I rededicated my life to him X number of years ago." I think God is most concerned with whether you are serving Him today. I do hope that over the years you have grown spiritually and continue to grow and mature as a believer.

Does faith come from hearing the Word of God or from reading the Word of God?

The context for your question comes from Romans 10. Contextually, that Scripture refers to preaching to the unbeliever. When the unbeliever hears the Word of the Lord, faith is made available. If he receives what he is hearing, he can be born again by confessing that Jesus Christ has been raised from the dead and is Lord of all.

Answer this question: Is your faith built up when you read the Word? The more you read about the goodness of God, the more your faith increases. As you read, you feed on it; it feeds your spirit and soul. So whether you are reading it, listening to it, or meditating on it, it has the power to build faith. But to keep the context, faith for salvation comes when a person hears the message about Christ.

If Christ is our Righteousness, then how can we still be judged if he was found guilty for us and paid the price in full?

If you are genuinely saved and have accepted Christ as your Lord, you are not going to be judged – not in that way. "There is therefore now no condemnation for those who are in Christ Jesus" (Romans 8:1). That word "condemnation" in Greek is *judgment*. There is no judgment for those who are in Christ Jesus. When you are saved, Christ considers you innocent. It's like a judge saying you are not guilty. From there, you start living the Christian life.

Since you have been saved, have you ever sinned? Yes, all of us have. Once we are saved, we are saved. But after we get saved, we all fall short. We all stumble in many ways (see James 3), but we are not going to be judged for salvation.

In other words, every time you sin, you don't have to think, *Uh-oh, I'm not saved any more; I have to get saved again. Oops! I sinned again; I need to get saved again...* No, you are saved! But you have to learn to walk in righteousness and sanctification.

If you are living in blatant, habitual, continual sin, you will never enter the Kingdom of God. There is a difference. If Jesus is your Lord and you are struggling with sin, should you die, you are still going to go to Heaven. Please understand that, but get out of the sin (see Hebrews 12:1-12).

CHAPTER 17

Understanding Prophecy

Please explain Daniel's vision in Daniel 8:16-26. Is this after or before Jesus died on the cross?

Daniel's vision gives a history of world powers before they came into being.

The Babylonians took captive the Southern kingdom of Judah in 605 B.C. and again in 597 B.C., with the final conquest and destruction of Jerusalem in 586 B.C. The Medo-Persian Empire then defeated the Babylonians, and the Greeks later defeated the Medo-Persians.

Chapter 8 of Daniel describes the incredible rise of the Greeks under the leadership of Alexander the Great and the overthrow of the two horned ram (the Medo-Persians). The he-goat (Alexander) has a horn on its head and is running so fast that its feet are not touching the ground. This is a reference to Alexander the Great and his rapidly expanding empire.

At a very young age, and in a phenomenal amount of time, Alexander conquers the world; however, while he is still young, at about age thirty-four or so, he dies either from syphilis or alcoholism or a combination of the two. (There are a few theories regarding his death.) In Daniel's prophecy, the goat's horn is broken off and four other horns spring up. The new horns represent Alexander's four generals and the empires they would create.

Let's continue looking at the prophecy as it unfolded. When Alexander lay dying, someone asked him, "Who will inherit your kingdom?"

He answered, "Give it to the strong. It goes to the one who can win it."

His four generals began what we might call a turf war. One general took area to the far west over by Rome, another took the region of Turkey, and one general, Ptolemy, established himself down in the area of Egypt. The fourth general took area to the north of Israel around Syria which later became the powerful

Seleucid Dynasty.   Antiochus IV Epiphanes eventually became ruler of this prevailing kingdom. He wreaked havoc on Jerusalem and attempted to annihilate the Jews and any signs, symbols, and practices of their religion.   The story is found in detail in *The Apocrypha*. It is the story of the Maccabees who stood their ground for eighty years. The Jews held firm against Antiochus and kept control of Israel until Rome became the dominant power force and conquered the region.   Rome was in power up until the time of Christ and beyond. This is what Daniel was shown and what he wrote down.

The prophecy is completely accurate to the effect that cynical higher critics of Bible interpretation balk at the validity of the prophecy. They charge that a historian must have written the information – that someone had to be looking back on a series of events and writing about them. Their thought is that no one could have been so accurate regarding what was going to happen in the future of human history.

The Bible accurately prophesies events before they ever come to pass. There is no other book on the planet that does that. When Jesus came, He fulfilled over three hundred prophecies given about Him in the Old Testament. The Bible is no ordinary book. It is separate from all other books.

How do you handle or talk to people who almost always say, "This is from the Lord," or "The Lord told me to do this," or "The Lord told me to share this," just so they can get their way which, many times, may not be of the Lord at all?

Isn't it interesting that you usually only find this practiced in Pentecostal and Charismatic circles? Please remember that I am a Charismatic myself. (Charismatic Christians believe the gifts of the Spirit are for today and were not limited to the time of the Apostles. We believe in the work of the Holy Spirit and that God still works miracles.)

I always take it as suspect when someone declares that the Lord told him this, or the Lord told her that. I have observed people do this to get their way. When it is truly from God, it will line up with Scripture. God is not going to tell anyone something that opposes His Word. The Spirit and the Word ALWAYS line up. If someone often says, "The Lord told me..." and then things don't work out or turn out as stated, that person begins to lose credibility. So the basic question would be: Does it line up with Scripture?

Sometimes it is difficult to discern one's own emotions and desires. Sometimes people do not want to take responsibility for their actions or lack thereof. These people will attach God's name to what they are doing when in reality they are doing what they choose to do. God does not override one's free will, and He does not contradict His Word.

Some people can say, "The Lord told me," and they are very well-meaning, albeit misguided. Others can be very manipulative in trying to convince you that the Lord told them something.

You have to be wise, and you have to be discerning. Don't simply swallow everything someone tells you because they put God's name on it. Read the Word, pray, and get wise counsel. The Bible does say that those led by the Spirit of God are the children of God (Romans 8:14). God can and does still speak to us, but you must be discerning.

Please give a modern day interpretation of Jeremiah 33 – the entire chapter, please.

Let's take a look at the historical setting before we bring it into a modern day application or understanding. Any time you read a prophecy in the Old Testament, you have to take into account what the specific Word was and to whom it was given.

The Assyrians had invaded the Northern Kingdom of Israel in 722 B.C., captured the inhabitants, and carted them off to Assyria. The Israelites were not well treated by the conquering army. Although the Assyrians conquered the Northern Kingdom, they did not venture all the way down into the Southern Kingdom.

God was patient. He prophesied through Isaiah and other prophets imploring the Israelites of the Southern Kingdom to listen to His voice. The prophets told the people they needed to repent and change their sinful ways, or God was going to allow another nation to come in and take them captive.

Jeremiah wrote around 600 B.C. Jeremiah prophesied right up to the day of the Israelites' captivity. The Word of the Lord to Jeremiah for the Israelites was that this captivity was going to come quickly. He basically gave them the following message from the Lord: "My mind is made up. You are going to be taken captive. You are going to be taken to a foreign land in Babylon (Iraq). For seventy years you will be held captive there, but I love you and will not forget you. I am going to bring you back. You will once again inhabit houses here and own land here. Because My love for you is great, I will return you back to your country."

Take a look at Daniel, Chapter 9. In Daniel 9, Daniel is writing in their sixty-seventh year of captivity. He says, "According to Jeremiah, we are going to be here seventy years. It's been sixty-seven years. We've got to get ready to go back; we've got to repent." Daniel gets on his knees and begins to pray. He stretches out his hands before the Lord and intercedes and repents for the nation. He tells the people it is time to get right before the Lord because God is about to send them all back to their homeland.

Well, they do get back to their native soil and under Ezra's reign begin to intermarry with foreign people who do not serve God. As a result, they begin turning away from the Lord once again. (Jeremiah's prophecy occurred seventy years before Ezra.)

So, Jeremiah 33 is speaking specifically to the nation of Israel. Jeremiah lets the people know that destruction is coming, but they will eventually return from captivity and go back to their lands. Daniel and Ezra give us glimpses of events that occur during their captivity and eventual release. How does it apply to us? Well, if you want to apply or interpret it in a personal way, it means that when you repent, and God's time of correcting or disciplining you is completed, He will return you to a time of blessing. The wise thing to do is to repent, return to the Lord, and receive His blessings.

It was told to me that all prophecy in the new covenant must be positive, and there must be no gloom and doom type prophecy. I was also told that prophecy that is negative is false prophecy. Is that true?

There are two different types of prophecy. There is predictive prophecy which is used to tell coming events, and there is inner-body (meaning within the church body) prophecy which is used as support to an individual or the entire local congregation.

Predictive prophecy is when someone speaks by the Spirit of the Lord and describes events that are going to happen in the future. In fact, the book of Revelation is prophetic, and it reveals some very negative coming events for mankind and for the future of the world. In the Book of Acts, a prophet named Agabus told of a coming famine (Acts 11:28). He also prophesied to Paul. Agabus took Paul's belt and tied his own hands and feet with it. He told Paul that in the same way he had tied his own hands and feet, the Jews would bind Paul and hand him over to the Gentiles (see Acts 21:10-11). This is predictive prophecy; it can be positive or negative.

The other kind of prophecy is inner-body prophecy. It offers encouragement for the body: building people up, comforting them in the faith, and sharing something the Spirit of the Lord is revealing in order to strengthen them. Why would a prophecy offer encouragement? Why comfort? And why building up? The devil, the world, and people discourage you. They tear you down and they dis-comfort you. When you come to the house of God and someone prophesies over you from God's Spirit to your spirit, it will encourage you and build you up. It will fortify you and comfort you in the faith. It's not predictive; it's encouraging, reassuring, and strengthening.

We see both types of prophecy in the New Testament.

CHAPTER 18

Biblical Knowledge and Understanding Scripture

Approximately how many times has the Bible been translated, and wouldn't that seem to alter some of the teachings?

There is manuscript evidence that proves the veracity of the Scriptures. What does manuscript evidence mean? It means hand-written documents – actual copies! There are more manuscript, hand-written copies of the New Testament than any ten pieces of literature on Earth. I think the closest to it is *The Iliad* by Homer; there are about six hundred and sixty copies of that. There are approximately twenty-four thousand reproductions of the New Testament that have been hand copied. Do we have the original documents that the Apostles wrote? No, we don't, but the original manuscripts have been copied and recopied. The greatest thing about the reproductions is that they contain only the slightest variations. For instance, one copy might say, "...and the Lord Jesus Christ," and another might say, "...and the Lord Christ Jesus." There's nothing altered in regard to doctrine or facts. Those who copied were extremely fastidious and studious with their copying to make sure there were no errors at all.

A Jewish scribe was so meticulous in copying the Old Testament laws that if he made an error, he would destroy the document and start all over again. That's why the Dead Sea Scrolls (which are over a thousand years old and were discovered in the 1900's) matched almost perfectly with our translation of the book of Isaiah today. It demonstrates how careful the scribes were. We have not lost anything in the translation. If you are going to discount the New Testament, then you are going to have to discount all of historical literature.

What about the missing books of the Bible which were not included in the Protestant Bible? Are those books not inspired by God also?

The inter-Testamental years between Malachi and Matthew are also called the silent years. During this time there were other writings by the Jews, and these writings are considered historical and factual. In the early fourth century, theologians and biblical scholars decided that these other writings were not what we would call *truly inspired* and were not to be incorporated into the scriptural books that make up our Bible. As a result, they were not included in the Canon of Scripture in the Protestant Bible. You can pick up a copy of *The Apocrypha* and read these texts. They are good reading, and there is some good history; however, in Protestant theology, scholars and theologians did not find that there was anything in them that added to the rest of the Word of God.

I would like to know how many brothers and sisters Jesus had and what their names were.

We don't know his sisters' names because the Bible does not tell us. It does tell us he had four brothers: James, Simon, Joseph, and Jude. Mark 6:3 says the people asked, "Isn't this the carpenter? Isn't this Mary's son and the brother of James, Joseph, Judas and Simon? Aren't his sisters here with us?" Scripture is very clear that Jesus did have siblings. (See also 1 Corinthians 9:5 and Matthew 12:46.)

Wasn't Mary Magdalene an apostle? Where can we find her writings?

No, Mary Magdalene was not an apostle. However, Jesus did cast seven demons out of her, and she became a devoted follower of Christ. If you looked, you would probably find something on the internet that says she was an apostle because you can find just about anything on the internet. However, whether it is valid or not is another issue.

She was not an apostle. She was a follower and a supporter of Jesus. She had no writings.

In Genesis 5, it says that Seth lived 912 years, Enosh lived 905 years, Kenan lived 910 years, Mahalalel lived 895 years, and Jared lived 962 years. In Genesis 9, it says that Noah lived 950 years. Did these people and others throughout the Bible really live to be this old or was tracking time back then different than it is now?

No, those are actual years. There was a canopy over the earth at that time, and there was no rain. The atmosphere was perfect, so the aging process was dramatically slowed down. God allowed people to live that long so they could populate the earth. He also gave mankind an opportunity to call out to Him and worship Him. Instead, they turned away from God, and He shortened their years to 120. He shortened man's years again to 70-80 and longer for some if they have the strength (see Psalm 90:9-10).

When Jesus went to the desert to fast for forty days and forty nights, where was the desert located and is it still there?

Yes, the desert is still there. It is down by old Jericho, and it is a very desolate and uninhabitable place. There are extremely dangerous cliffs from which you can see for a long distance. You can visit the area when you travel to the Holy Land.

Someone asked me if there was anything in the New Testament about prostitution. I am not sure why he asked, but I told him about some Old Testament passages and about Mary Magdalene in the New Testament. Other than that, are there any other places where the New Testament talks about it?

Remember, prostitution is one of the oldest occupations on the planet. It has always been around; it will always be around. You have heard the saying "sex sells." As long as there is sinful humanity, there will be prostitution, immorality, drug addiction and alcoholism, robbery, thievery, murder, lying, and all such sinful

217

practices. So, yes, in that sense, it was prolific in New Testament times.

In the Old Testament, we have the stories of Rahab and others. In the New Testament, Paul warns against uniting ones body with a prostitute, so we know that prostitution was very much in existence during that time (1 Corinthians 6:16). Jesus said that prostitutes were getting into the Kingdom ahead of the religious leaders because the prostitutes repented, and the religious leaders did not (Matthew 21:31; see Matthew 21: 28-32).

Jesus was here on earth over two thousand years ago. Do we know how long ago Adam and Eve were here?

There are two schools of thought regarding the age of the earth: New Earth Theory and Old Earth Theory.

New Earth Theory says that if you literally recount time using the Bible dates, you can biblically trace the age of the earth. For example, this person lived this long and begat the next person. The next person lived so many years and begat so many children, and so on. New Earth scholars believe the earth is between six and seven thousand years old from the time God created it.

Old Earth scholars believe there is a gap of time between Genesis 1:1 and Genesis 1:2 where it says, "In the beginning God created the heavens and the earth." – GAP – "Now the earth was formless and empty, darkness was over the surface of the deep, and the Spirit of God was hovering over the waters." These scholars believe there is a definite time rupture, and the gap allows space and time for an old earth. They don't know how long that gap was.

Some Christians support the scientific views of the Old Earth Theory, while others take a literal interpretation of the Genesis account of creation, and agree with the New Earth scholars.

What is a good way to memorize the order of the books of the Bible? I have to go back and forth looking for specific books because I cannot seem to memorize them in order.

In Bible college we had to memorize them, and you did whatever you could to get them in your brain. Some people used a song; others got a rhythm going. There are many approaches you could take. I would suggest you start with the New Testament. One method is with repetition. Start with a few books, "Matthew, Mark, Luke, John." Repeat the phrase over and over until you get it. Then add another book or two "Matthew, Mark, Luke, John, Acts, Romans..." Keep it up for a few days or however long it takes you until you have them all memorized.

Another way is to relate the books to something – do you know someone named Matthew? Do you know someone named

Mark? Some people create a mental picture or map to help them remember. Others take the first letter of each word and make a sentence, for example – M (Matthew) – my, M (Mark) – mother, L (Luke) – likes, J (John) – jellybeans, etc.

Do whatever works for you. You'll get it. The main thing is to practice. Once you think you have the list committed to memory, continue repeating it from time to time until it really does become automatic. Keep coming to church, too! That will help.

Mark 10:31 says that many who seem to be important now will be least important then, what does this mean?

That's not exactly what it says. It says the first shall be last and the last shall be first. In Matthew's gospel (Matthew 20), the terms are reversed: The last will be first, and the first will be last. A parable precedes this phrase, which helps us understand what Jesus is saying.

The parable says that the kingdom of heaven is like a landowner who went out early in the morning and hired men to work on his property. He agreed to pay them a specific wage. A few hours later, the landowner went out again and saw others standing around. He hired them. Later, he went out and, again, hired more workers. Twice more he went out and saw others and hired them as well. Each group was hired later than the group before.

At the end of the day, all of the workers were called in and, beginning with those hired last, payment was disbursed. The later workers received the same pay as what had been promised to the early morning workers. When those who had been hired early in the day saw this, they expected to receive more. When they received the initially agreed upon amount, they became angry. The Bible says they grumbled against the landowner. The landowner reminded them that they had agreed to work for a certain amount and stated that he wished to pay those who came later the same wage, expressing the fact that he could be generous with his own money.

The point of the parable is this: We're all equal. We are all going to cross the threshold of heaven the same way. We get saved, and we all enter into heaven by the blood of Jesus Christ. We will all stand before the Lord, the first and the last, the last and the first.

When Cain was sent away, he was sealed by God so that no one else would hurt him. If Adam and Eve were the first people created, who were those people Cain was afraid of?

We have to remember that not only did Adam and Eve live many, many years ago, but they also lived to be over nine hundred years of age. They had other sons and daughters. As people began to populate, cousins grew into second and third cousins. God had to protect Cain because of what he had done; he had murdered his brother. Looking at it logically from Scripture, it would seem that the population multiplied and grew, so there were eventually many people on the planet. We don't know what the mark was, but it was a sign to all people that Cain was protected by God.

What is God saying in Jeremiah 35 where He talks about us not listening to Him?

In Jeremiah 35, we read about the Rekabites. They were a nomadic tribe who wandered the landscape and lived in tents, and they were a people of their word. When they gave their word, they kept their word. They had received instructions from their forbearers not to drink wine or build cities or plant crops, so they took vows to abstain from wine and to avoid certain aspects of life. They obeyed these commands, and they stood by what they promised.

God used the Rekabites as an illustration. He contrasted the Rekabites who listened to their forefathers with the chosen people of Israel who refused to listen to instruction. Numerous warnings had been given, but the people would not obey and turn from their wickedness. As a result, disaster was imminent.

Was it Moses or Abraham that God wanted to terminate?

God was going to kill Moses because he didn't circumcise his son. His wife ended up circumcising the child. When she did, she cast the foreskin at Moses' feet. She said, "You are a husband of blood to me." She was basically saying, "You should have done this." God was going to kill him for not doing it. Circumcision was the sign of the covenant between God and His chosen people, the Jews (Exodus 4: 24-26).

What was the meaning behind Christ's comment on the cross, "My God, My God, why have you forsaken me?"

Jesus became a sin offering. The Father had to allow the Son to pay the penalty for our sin. God took all of His wrath, all that was supposed to be on mankind, every sin from the beginning of time to the end of time, and placed it all on the Lord Jesus Christ, and the Father had to turn away. Jesus knew that. He felt God looking upon him with the same displeasure that He would have when He looks upon sinful man because on him (Christ) were all the sins of humanity, and he knew the Father turned away. It is difficult for us to comprehend.

Jesus did not sin and he did not become sin. The Bible says he became a sin offering, a substitute, an innocent sacrifice for the guilty. At that moment, God had to unleash His wrath, and

Jesus cried out, quoting a line from Psalm 22:1, "Eloi, Eloi lema sabachthani," which translates, "My God, My God, why have You forsaken me?" (Mark 15:34; Matthew 27:46.)

In the Bible there is a story of some Israelite men wanting to have sex with male guests who had visited a home. The hosts protected their guests and offered up their virgin daughters instead. What is that all about?

There are two similar incidents recorded in the Old Testament. One is found in Genesis 19 and the other in Judges 19.

In Genesis 19, Lot received two visitors into his home. Later that same evening, a mob surrounded his house and demanded the visitors be sent outside so the men of the city could have sex with them. Lot refused and offered his two virgin daughters instead. The two visitors (who were actually angels of the Lord sent to rescue Lot and his family from the destruction that was about to be poured out upon the city) pulled Lot inside and caused the crowd to become blind. The wicked men became confused and were unable to enter the house.

In Judges 19, a traveler, his servant, and his concubine were on their way to Jerusalem and stopped in Gibeah for the night. They needed a place to stay and, surprisingly, no one offered them lodging. Finally, an elderly man opened his home to them and, later that night, wicked men of the city came and began pounding on the door, demanding that the traveler be sent outside so they could have sex with him. The owner of the house refused and offered to send out his virgin daughter and the concubine. The traveler thrust his concubine outside, and the men sexually assaulted her through the night. The woman made her way back to the house only to die on the threshold.

What difficult and heart wrenching stories these are. They are very sad and strange and are challenging to our twenty-first century understanding.

It is a searing and confusing picture of a culture that honored hospitality over chivalry and gallantry. If you were a traveler passing through a city at night, you could sit in the city square where any of the townspeople would see you, and someone would usually offer to bring you in for the evening. If a family opened its home to you, you would be fed and given a place to rest and sleep. Your hosts were responsible for your welfare until your departure. Customarily, in that part of the world, a host family took very good care of guests who came into the household, even to the detriment of the family's own interests and safety.

The sexually perverted men in these cities demanded the hosts send their male visitors outside. The hosts felt their guests' lives were at stake and were willing to give up their virgin daughters (and a female concubine) and allow the men to rape the women instead. How very awful! We do not understand it, and it makes absolutely no sense to us. It is a dysfunctional kind of misguided loyalty in our eyes – that someone would take care of male guests and protect them at the cost of one's own family and other women in the home. Every time I read it, I'm extremely bothered by it. My thought is *just fight the guys at the door.*

Lot's daughters were saved because they were protected by the angelic travelers. The concubine in Judges 19 was not so fortunate. The man she traveled with had little regard for her care. It is a sad commentary on the lack of value or protection afforded women in certain sectors of society at that time.

We must look at passages like these within the entirety of Scripture. We are reminded that God's people are fallible human beings, subject to inappropriate and corrupt cultural traditions and norms. As believers today, we have to decide whether we will allow culture (be it secular culture, our ethnic culture, our family culture, or peer culture) and what culture deems appropriate to dictate right and wrong for us, or if we will allow God's Word to dictate our lives.

Please explain Matthew 5:32 where it says any man who marries a divorced woman commits adultery. Am I now an adulterer for the rest of my life?

That's a very interesting question and a very interesting passage. Jesus says God created man and woman, male and female. When the two become husband and wife, in the mind of God, they commit their lives in a covenant relationship, and that covenant cannot be broken. What God has joined together, no one can tear apart (Matthew 19:6).

Jesus said, "Moses permitted you to divorce your wives because your hearts were hard. But it was not this way from the beginning" (Matthew 19:8). Technically, Jesus stated that God does not honor divorce. If a person marries and then gets divorced and marries another person, he or she is committing adultery. That's a tough place to be.

It seems to mean that when you married this second person and consummated the marriage, you committed adultery. Without biblical grounds for divorce, remarriage to a new person is called an act of adultery because God did not validate the divorce. Divorce without biblical grounds is hardness of heart by one or both people.

Now, however, this second marriage has become viable, and you move forward together as one. Thank the Lord for His grace and mercy. You and your spouse, live out the rest of your days together honoring and serving Him.

In Luke 18:5 what kind of "troubling" was the unjust judge referring to?

It's a parable; Jesus was telling a story to teach us a lesson on prayer.

The story refers to an unjust judge who does not care about God and does not care about people. A widow comes to him and says, "Give me what is due me. Be fair to me."

The judge responds, "Be gone!"

She keeps coming to him, imploring him, "Give me what is due me!"

The judge says, "This woman is troubling me. Let me give her what she wants, lest she weary me." Jesus said that if an unjust judge will lend an ear and respond, how much more will God answer prayers for His children? So much more indeed!

The woman was nagging, bothering, and troubling the judge. It is an illustration for us to remain steadfast in prayer. If an unrighteous and unjust judge will relent, listen and respond, God who is absolutely righteous and just, and who is consistently acting in our behalf will so much more respond to us when we pray! Are we willing to be faithful and persistent in prayer, or do we easily give up, figuring that God probably will not respond?

It is an illustration that tells us to keep praying and seeking God until He answers us. This is what prayer is all about. Prayer is to be consistent. Don't give up. Ask, seek, and knock!

In Psalm 91 it says, "With your eyes you will see the reward of the wicked." What does that mean?

Remember to read the entire passage and always consider the context. In this passage, David is talking about fighting against his enemies and winning. The word "reward" here could equally mean punishment. The New International Version states it this way, "You will only observe with your eyes and will see the *punishment* of the wicked" (Psalm 91:8). God is promising David that he will see his enemies defeated. In this Psalm, David is actually prophesying. The wicked will receive their "reward" or what is due them, but it is not a good reward.

We do not wish eternal punishment on anyone, so it is vitally important for us to share the message and love of Christ with those who do not know him. At the same time, we cannot deny the truth of Scripture. The wicked will perish if they do not genuinely repent and seek God's forgiveness.

Where can I find the Scripture that refers to casting down imaginations?

2 Corinthians 10:4-5 says, "The weapons of our warfare are not carnal but mighty in God for the pulling down of strongholds, casting down arguments and every high thing that exalts itself

against the knowledge of God, bringing every thought into captivity to the obedience of Christ" (NKJV).

The King James Version of the Bible uses the word "imaginations" while the New King James Version and the New International Version use the word "arguments." It is a spiritual exercise that requires you to actively exalt the Word of God above your own doubts, lusts, and imaginations. It's about learning to stop the lies and deceptions of the enemy and retrain your thinking to focus on the truth of the Scriptures. It requires practice of and submission to God's Word and authority. Above all, it requires recognition that God's Word is true.

What does it mean to not bear false witness against your neighbor?

Not bearing false witness means we do not lie against, about, or to our neighbor. "False" implies that you are not going to tell the truth about something. A false witness could be as specific as someone in court. For example, you are a witness and you are going to "bear witness" to what you know happened or didn't happen. Overall, it is a commandment not to lie, slander, or share untruths about someone in any situation.

Pastor, per your understanding of Scripture, what would you say is the role of women in the church? Can women be pastors, teachers, and evangelists?

According to the Word of God, I do not see any place in the New Testament where a woman is to be an elder or the lead pastor of a church. So, if someone says it is okay, I would not agree. There are anointed women speakers, and the Bible says that as long as they're not usurping authority or position, it is okay. God has commissioned the men to be the leaders of the congregation. Sorry, it's not a popular stance; however, that's my interpretation of 1 Timothy 2 and 1 Corinthians 14.

Where in the Bible does it say that in the last days you will not be able to determine the seasons?

That's not what it says. The Pharisees and Sadducees came to test Jesus and asked that He show them a sign from heaven. He rebuked them saying they could determine the weather according to the signs of the sky, but they were unable to discern the signs of the times. They could read the seasons but could not see the hand of God moving in their generation. It is found in Matthew 16.

Please explain the verse that says, "I will put before them a stumbling block." What is a stumbling block?"

The passage comes out of the eighth chapter of Isaiah. God was raising up the nation of Assyria to punish the Israelites. God spoke to Isaiah instructing him not to listen to the people around him who were turning away from the Lord but to turn to the Lord and fear and reverence Him, for the Lord would be a stumbling block to the people. God's people knew to do right but chose to do wrong. By continually living against God, they would stumble and fall over His commands.

It was a contrast. If you are following God, He becomes your cornerstone and everything else in life is built on His foundation. He is your "Rock." However, if you are running away from or against God, you are going to stumble over Him again and again. His precepts and His truth will constantly be areas of life in which you will harden your heart. In the end, you will come to deeply regret rejecting Him.

Did Jesus exist in Heaven before the manger? If so, where in tho Bible does it say so?

Yes, Jesus existed before the manger. He most definitely existed. Here are a few scriptures that verify Christ's pre-existence:

- *But you, Bethlehem Ephrathah, though you are small among the clans of Judah, out of you will come for me one who will be ruler over Israel, whose origins are from old, from ancient times* (Micah 5:2). (Some translations read, "*from eternity.*")

- *In the beginning was the Word, and the Word was with God, and the Word was God. He was with God in the beginning. Through him all things were made; without him nothing was made that has been made* (John 1:1-3).

- Jesus says, "*And now Father, glorify me in your presence with the glory I had with you before the world began*" (John 17: 5).

- *In the past God spoke to our ancestors through the prophets at many times and in various ways, but in these last days he has spoken to us by his Son, whom he appointed heir of all things, and through whom also he made the universe* (Hebrews 1:1-2).

- *The Son is the image of the invisible God, the firstborn over all creation. For in him all things were created: things in heaven and on earth, visible and invisible, whether thrones or powers or rulers or authorities; all things have been created through him and for him* (Colossians 1: 15-16).

- In John 17:24, Jesus says to his Father God, *"...you loved me before the creation of the world."*

I know the number 666 has something to do with the devil. How did that come about?

In Revelation 13, we read about the coming of the beast and the power of the anti-Christ. The beast will deceive the whole earth with peace, and he will make everyone take a mark on the forehead or on the wrist. Whoever does not have the mark cannot buy and sell.

Think about it for a moment. The mark will be needed to purchase food, water, and daily necessities. It will be required in order for an individual to fully operate in society. This will be a terrible time, especially for Christians. In the next chapter, the outcome gets even worse. Revelation 14 says that whoever takes the mark of the beast will be cut off from the Lord.

As for the number 666, no one seems to be exactly sure what it specifically stands for. It is associated with the Beast and identifies his name or his number (Revelation 13:18). Seven is the number of God and perfection, while six is man's number. All of humanity falls short of God's perfect holiness.

Here is the question I would ask you right now – If you cannot live for the Lord now, and we do go through the tribulation, how will you ever die for Him when your very life will be required of you?

Did giants really come down to have relations with human women on earth?

Chapter six of Genesis says, "The sons of God saw that the daughters of men were beautiful and they married any of them they chose" (Genesis 6:2). It seems that the offspring were giants; however, that isn't exactly what it says. There are a few views on this passage.

One explanation holds that "sons of God" refers to godly men, perhaps from the line of Seth, who married wicked women from the line of Cain. These relationships produced offspring that polluted the human race to the point where God had to destroy the earth in a flood because no one lived uprightly except for Noah and his family.

Another explanation is that the term "sons of God" could mean sons of nobility who were often elevated to godlike stature among their people. These men would have been corrupt leaders who did not fear God.

The most accepted view is that "sons of God" refers to angels who abandoned their obedient positions as God's messengers and followed Satan. They came to earth to possess men, mated with women, and had children who were a hybrid of both angelic and human offspring in order to contaminate the human race. It was because of this pollution that God destroyed the earth in a flood and started over with Noah's family. This is the view held in Judaism and by the early church fathers. The Hebrew term is "Bené Elohim" or "Sons of God" and almost always refers to angels in the Bible.

The giants, however, were already on the earth, and these people groups reappear even after the flood. Remember Goliath? He came from a people group who were physically large.

I do not understand Ecclesiastes 7:15-18. Would you please explain this passage?

Ecclesiastes 7:15-18 is a very interesting passage. It says, "In this meaningless life of mine I have seen both of these: the righteous perishing in their righteousness, and the wicked living long in their wickedness. Do not be over righteousness, neither be over wise – why destroy yourself? Do not be over wicked, and do not be a fool – why die before your time? It is good to grasp the one, and not let go of the other. Whoever fears God will avoid all extremes."

It's a warning not to be overly legalistic about everything, thinking you can't do this or you can't do that. Some Christians think there is no fun involved in being a believer. They walk around sour faced and finding fault with everyone and everything. On the other side, there is the admonition not to be so free in your Christianity that you're stepping into sinful practices and habits that you have no business being involved in. Some Christians take the liberty they have in Christ and use that liberty to live sinful lives.

So, don't be legalistic and don't be loose in your living. Keep a balance. Read Romans 14; it will help you to understand that passage better.

What is the best explanation for Mark 13 where it says that no one knows the day or the hour, not the angels, nor the Son, only the Father?

Mark 13:32 says, "But of that day or hour no one knows, not even the angels in heaven, nor the Son, but only the Father."

"That day" is a term for the day of the Lord's appearance and is a reference to Christ's return. Remember, in coming to earth as a man, Jesus emptied himself of being only God and took on humanity, and he fully submitted to his Father's will. In his human state, he could not operate fully as God. For instance, he could only physically be in one place at one time; he slept, he ate, he drank, he got tired, etc.

Jesus said only the Father knows when the Son is going to come back; not even the Son knows. This is very Jewish. In Jewish culture, a young man would not take a bride until his father said that the bride and the husband-to-be were ready. Following along those Jewish cultural lines, Jesus was in essence saying, "My Father will let me know when my bride is ready for me to go and pick her up." What an exciting day that will be for all believers.

What does the Bible say about hereditary illness? Are God's people subject to biology and genetics from unsaved parents?

You are made up of cells that you inherited from your parents, grandparents, and great-grandparents whether they were saved or unsaved. Your genetic code, the DNA in your body, was passed down to you through heredity. So, if your father was bald and your grandfather was bald, guess what? Your chances of becoming bald are higher than someone who comes from a family where baldness is rare. If your family line is prone to high cholesterol or diabetes or cancer, then you want to live as healthy as you can because hereditary issues are propelled down through the gene pool. Mental illness can be passed down as well.

Regarding hereditary curses, we are born again believers, and we have the Spirit of God and the authority of Scripture. The power of God can break any curses that have been placed on a family.

At the end of the book of Ezra, those who married foreign women sent the wives and their kids back to their own countries. This seems the opposite of what Jesus said to do. God stays the same. Can you please give insight into this Old Testament event?

Let's first set the stage. The book of Ezra recounts the returning of the Jewish people to their homeland after being held in captivity for seventy years. As He had promised, God allowed them to go back to their own land. They traveled back home, settled down, built a wall around the city, and went back to trading, doing commerce, and worshiping the Lord.

As time went by, the men started marrying foreign women (women outside of the nation of Israel). Doing so was against God's commands, and this same sin was one of the reasons they lost their homeland years prior. The exclusion against marrying foreigners was a safeguard to protect them from outside influences that would draw them away from the Lord and toward idolatry.

We could compare their return home to being on parole. Here's what I mean: Let's say you get out of jail after serving a five year sentence. You are on parole, but then you begin to go right back to the same friends you used to run with. You begin selling the same drugs that you used to sell. One of your buddies sees you and says, "What are you thinking, man? You need to stay away from that crowd. Don't you see how you're being drawn back into your old lifestyle? Get rid of those people and that stuff or you're going to get put away for good this time."

In the same way, Ezra saw that the people were marrying individuals from other nations, and he saw the potential of their being lured away from the Lord God. He said (paraphrased), "Look, we cannot do this. This sin is what turned our hearts from the Lord in the first place and caused us to be exiled for seventy years. Those of you who have joined yourselves with foreigners need to let the foreign women go, even if they have your kids, because God told us not to intermarry with other nations and not to let our lives become entwined with non-Israelites and their gods." Ezra admonished the people because they had been unfaithful to God and by their wrongdoing had added to the guilt of the Nation. As a result, the Israelites wrote the non-Israelites certificates of divorce and sent them away. Each case was examined individually, and the process took three months to complete.

God has not changed. He had given His people very specific instructions regarding how to live and how to keep themselves pure before Him. Remember, pagan foreigners brought foreign gods, foreign practices, and idol worship. When you marry someone, his or her ways slowly creep into your ways. God had set His people apart and wanted their hearts turned toward Him, not toward idols and foreign gods.

Am I correct in believing that when a person becomes a born again Christian, in that moment, God gives him the gift of the Holy Spirit?

Every believer who truly gives his or her heart to Christ and sincerely confesses that Jesus Christ is Lord receives the Holy Spirit. The Spirit of God comes to dwell within that person. The Spirit is a seal of belonging, a deposit assuring that God is coming back for His people. The Spirit is a guarantee that one belongs to the Lord. Every true believer receives the Holy Spirit. Read Romans 8:9-16 and Ephesians 1:13-14.

I heard someone say that Paul describes Jesus' looks as a person you wouldn't consider hanging out with since he was not very good looking like the pictures and statues show him to be. Where can I find this?

Paul did not say this; the Scripture you are thinking of is Isaiah 53:2. Isaiah prophesied that one would come up from the line of David, and there would be nothing in his appearance that would draw us to him. He wouldn't have a beautiful face or remarkable looks or any of those characteristics that attract others. There would be nothing in his physical appearance that would make humanity blindly follow him. It was who he was and what he spoke, the things he did, and the compassion that came out of his heart that drew people to Christ.

241

Was Jesus a Jew or a Christian?

Define a Christian for me. Who does a Christian follow? Christ, of course. A Christ-ian is a Christ follower. Jesus is the cornerstone of Christianity. He was born a Jew, born under the law. He lived the Jewish faith, but he came to mankind offering the Father's kingdom to all. He brought a new covenant, revealing the spirit of the law rather than the letter of the law. The letter of the law kills, but the Spirit of God gives life.

Jesus brings life to all who accept him. He was Jewish and was the basis for the foundation of Christianity.

I know that God is our Heavenly Father. Do we have a Heavenly Mother?

No, we do not have a heavenly mother. God is Spirit; He is not begotten. He has always been in existence and always will be. Jesus is also Spirit. He is eternal. However, he had to have an earthly mother to give birth to his physical body. His physical body was to carry him around on earth so he could offer himself as a sacrifice on the cross. The Bible does not mention a heavenly mother in that sense. It knows no such thing. In Galatians 4:26, Paul states, "But the Jerusalem that is above is free, and she is our mother." Keep it in context – Paul is stating that Christians are citizens of the heavenly city of God.

When Jesus went to the high mountain to be transfigured, what did Moses and Elijah represent?

We read in Matthew 17, Mark 9, and Luke 9, that Jesus went up on what's come to be known as the Mount of Transfiguration. While he was up there, Moses and Elijah appeared. In the Old Testament, the Law and the Prophets pointed to and spoke of the coming Messiah. Moses represents the Law, and Elijah represents the Prophets. Christ is the Messiah, the bringer of the new covenant. In this brief snapshot on the mountain, we are given a picture of the Law, the Prophets, and Jesus who is the fulfillment of the Old Testament law and prophecies.

Peter was not allowed to tell anyone about the event until after Jesus rose from the dead (2 Peter 1:16-18). Remember, Peter was up on that mountain, and he saw Moses, Elijah, and Jesus together. Peter says they spoke about Christ's leaving and that his time on earth was coming to a close. Jesus was getting ready to go to the cross. Everything that was written about the Messiah in the law and the prophets was about to be fulfilled.

Of all the Nazirite vows that Samson broke, why do you think he kept the one about not cutting his hair?

First of all, he did not keep the one of not cutting his hair. Samson knew his hair held the secret to his strength. God told him that he

243

would remain strong if he did not cut his hair or drink or eat anything from the vine. However, Samson allowed himself to be put in a compromising position. He saw trouble but refused to ignore it. He saw what he knew was a trap and kept right on walking into it. Foolishly, he played with temptation and sin instead of making up his mind to go in a different direction. The enemy used a person to deceive him, and she got him to give up the very source of his power.

Does that sound familiar? We see the signs; we know it's dangerous, but we figure we can handle it. We figure we are strong enough. We live on the edge. It was foolishness on Samson's part, and I pray that you will exercise the wisdom that he did not. He had the knowledge to act differently but chose foolishness, and it cost him his life. Seemingly small decisions can have excruciating consequences.

Could you explain binding and loosing as stated in Matthew 16 and 18?

In Pentecostal circles, it is often taken to mean that in prayer a person can bind the devil and loose faith and blessing into one's circumstances, but is this interpretation true to the context of these verses?

Context always determines meaning. Always consider Scripture in its context. In Matthew 16, Jesus is talking to Peter. Peter has just declared Jesus as the Christ. Jesus states that on this rock, on this truth, he will build his church, and the gates of hell will not be able to prevail against it. Jesus then says, "I will give you the keys of the kingdom of heaven; whatever you bind on earth will be bound in heaven, and whatever you loose on earth will be loosed in heaven" (Matthew 16:19).

Many scholars believe it is a reference to church discipline. The Jewish rabbis had the authority to pass binding decisions – they could declare something forbidden or permissible and the people had to adhere to the instructions. The Apostles were the first preachers. In the same sense, they established for us the words of Christ and the application of the Scriptures.

One interpretation is that Jesus is giving the church authority to bind men's sins to them or release them. In other words, the church has been given the right to declare persons guilty or innocent.

In Matthew 18 Jesus discusses how to deal with someone who has offended you. You first approach the person one-on-one. If the matter is not resolved, then you take two or three people with you to have a conversation with the person. If, after that, you are still unable to work things out, you then bring the elders of the church to speak with the individual. After these steps have been followed, if there is no true resolution, you can walk away from the person. Following this discourse, Jesus says, "Truly I tell you, whatever you bind on earth will be bound in heaven, and whatever you loose on earth will be loosed in heaven" (Matthew 18:18). Again, the context applies to properly dealing with members of the body.

Both contexts seem to relate binding and loosing to forgiveness and releasing people. You can stretch the phrase to mean more than that, but you would be taking it out of its contextual setting.

What is the difference between grace and favor?

They are pretty close to being synonymous. Grace is unmerited favor. Unmerited means it cannot be earned. It is given as a gift. Favor includes grace, but favor also suggests selective partiality. God can choose to have favor on anyone in particular, just as you can choose to demonstrate favor toward someone. We want both grace and favor from God. Grace is included in favor, and favor is included in grace.

Please explain what books and Scriptures were left out of the Bible and why.

The Protestant Bible has sixty-six books, while the Catholic Bible has additional books called *The Apocrypha*. The books of *The Apocrypha* contain some history, and the information is considered factual; however, when the canon (the standard, the norm) of Scripture was closed with sixty-six books, twenty-seven in the New Testament and thirty-nine in the Old Testament, the Apocryphal books were not included. They were, however, included in the Catholic canon of Scriptures.

My ten year old son's friends were questioning him about his faith. He held his ground but got stuck when they began asking him about cavemen. When did cavemen come in to the picture, and how do they relate in regard to Adam and Eve's story? How can I explain it to him?

The theory of evolution was started by mankind. The caveman hypothesis is a concept developed in human minds to substantiate the belief in an evolutionary system. The theory is that man was once an ape and ultimately evolved to become a human being. At some point he began to live in caves and continued evolving to become modern man.

The closest thing we have to cavemen in biblical history is that some people actually lived in caves. Even modern-day

247

cultures have lived in caves but not in the evolutionary sense that Darwin asserted. Biblically, God created man: Adam and Eve, male and female He created them. You can look up *Genesis.org* and research more information on the subject. The evolutionary thesis of Darwin was presented in direct opposition to the Word of God. Evolution is not based on factual information; it's a theory.

Why did Job and others in the Bible shave their heads?

Job and others shaved their heads as a sign of grief, humility, and sorrow. People would tear their clothes, throw dust in the air, and shave off their beards as an expression of incredible heartache or distress. Sometimes it was done in reaction to a negative situation or as an expression of great repentance or remorse.

Would you agree that one of the greatest needs in the pulpit is the faithful exposition of the Scriptures, and one of the greatest needs in the pews is biblical literacy?

Yes, absolutely. The greatest need in the pulpit is for preachers to stand up and expound the Word of God. It is the preacher's responsibility to explain the Scriptures so the people can better understand the Bible. The greatest need of the congregation is not solely biblical literacy but also biblical understanding and application of the knowledge that has been learned. We are called to be doers of the Word, not simply hearers. Teaching, learning, and application go hand in hand.

I can teach and teach and teach, but if I don't allow the Holy Spirit to be in control, then my teaching is in vain, and we are simply an empty, biblically-educated congregation. My job as a shepherd is to teach, guide, lead, and mentor as I depend on God. Your job is to learn, grow, and then become teachers yourselves – guiding, leading, and mentoring others.

We must know the Word, apply its teachings to our hearts and lives, and grow in wisdom, knowledge, and understanding. As we do this, we grow in love for God and for each other, and this love will be demonstrated in our actions.

Does everyone who speaks in tongues speak the same dialect?

The Bible addresses the issue of tongues in 1 Corinthians 12, 13, and 14. It says that there are earthly tongues and there are heavenly tongues, and all of them are significant. There are tongues that are human languages (other people somewhere in the world can understand them when they are spoken) and tongues that are angelic (tongues we cannot understand).

Just listen as two individuals pray or speak in tongues. You can tell that they are not speaking the same dialect or language. The languages usually don't sound anything alike. That is, of course, unless you go to a class on speaking in tongues, and the instructor tells you that the way to speak in tongues is to speak really fast saying, "She rode on my Honda," or "I tie my bow tie." If everyone comes out of the class sounding exactly alike, then there's a problem.

Speaking in tongues is not simply speaking really quickly or just babbling. We can pretend to be speaking in tongues, but the true gift of tongues is from God. So, to answer your question, no, not all "tongues" or languages from the Spirit are the same.

In Acts 20:16-18, Paul speaks of a time he spent in Asia. What region of the world is he talking about? Is it the Asia we know today?

During the time of Paul's writing, Rome controlled the world, and within its domain was a place called Asia Minor or Roman Asia. It is the area to which the seven letters in the book of Revelation are written. Paul was forbidden to go there on his second missionary journey (Acts 16:6). However, he did travel to that region on his third missionary journey, and he preached the Gospel message throughout the area for three years. So, no, it is not the Asia that we know of today; it would be the area of modern-day Turkey.

In 2 Corinthians 12, Paul says he knows a man who was caught up into Paradise and who heard inexpressible words which are not lawful for a man to utter. Who is the man Paul is speaking of?

We believe Paul is speaking about himself because he clarifies it later. He goes on to state that he received a thorn in the flesh to keep him from becoming prideful because of the surpassing revelations he experienced. From this internal evidence (evidence within the text), we understand that Paul is talking about himself.

What does Paul mean in 2 Corinthians 12, when he talks about the third heaven?

There are three heavens in traditional Jewish theology. There is the atmosphere that surrounds us; it is the air we breathe, where the birds fly, etc. There is the atmosphere where the planets are, and then there is the atmosphere where the throne of God is. Paul said he had a revelation in which he actually went to the third heaven and saw things he did not know how to express or explain. Also, he was not permitted to share what he saw. What did he see? Your guess is as good as mine. Many theologians have guessed at what he saw, but no one really knows.

251

How does one grieve the Holy Spirit?

Disobedience grieves the Holy Spirit, and the Bible tells us not to grieve the Holy Spirit (Ephesians 4: 30). We are to obey what He's prompting, what He's saying, and what the Word says. Remember, the Word and the Spirit always line up. Do not grieve (sadden, hurt) the Holy Spirit by disobedience.

Was the fact that King David had many wives a sin?

Yes, it was. God told the kings not to take many wives. God made an allowance for it because the Israelites fell into the trap of the nations around them. God's original plan was for one man to be united with one woman. He has not changed.

One reason the kings of Israel took more than one wife was so they could have many children, especially boys. Having boys would ensure that the king would have successors to the throne after him. It was also considered a sign of virility and authority, and sometimes a marriage may have been a political move as well. Does any of that mean it was the God-honoring thing to do? No.

Is it a gift of God to be slain in the Spirit?

If it is genuinely God who wants to knock you down, then He is going to knock you down. Sometimes people have been pushed down, or some might get caught up in the emotion of people falling down and think they ought to fall down as well. We do not condone or want any of those kinds of suspicious things going on in our local assembly. We want God's presence. If God wants to lay you on the ground and tickle you while you're down there, that's fine with me, but it's got to be of God.

It's very easy to get emotionally excited and exhibit some bizarre behavior and attach God's name to it. Then we get offended if anyone questions whether or not the experience was really God. Think about this, if it was really God, would you get offended by someone asking you about your experience?

I know that Moses, Aaron, Joshua, and Miriam were siblings. Did they have the same mother and father? Were there other siblings with the same parents?

Moses, Aaron, and Miriam were siblings and, as far as we know, had the same parents. Joshua was not their brother.

253

We all come from Adam and Eve, right? So, they had children and then their children slept together and so on? Isn't that incest? So, technically, we are all related?

According to the Bible, we all descended from one man – Adam. Adam and Eve had many children, and the book of Genesis tells the story of three of them – Cain, Abel, and Seth. Cain, the firstborn, killed his brother Abel. We know that Eve's childbearing did not end there. Genesis 5:4 says, "When Adam had lived 130 years, he had a son in his own likeness, in his own image; and he named him Seth. After Seth was born, Adam lived 800 years and had other sons and daughters. Altogether, Adam lived a total of 930 years, and then he died."

It was the beginning of human life on earth. It stands to reason that Adam and Eve had more children, many more. They were commanded to be fruitful and multiply. Cain, Abel, and Seth are the only three whose stories are told. For a time, and for the purpose of populating the planet, God allowed intermarriage between siblings, but this was only for a time. Later, during the time of Moses, strict laws were given forbidding the marriage of close relatives (Leviticus 18-20).

Remember, Adam and Eve were created in perfection. There were no physical defects or abnormalities. There was no contamination of the gene pool or mutations within DNA from close relatives marrying. Their offspring married each other for a time until that dispensation ended, and God no longer allowed it.

254

This topic can be a stumbling block for many Christians because we know that intermarriage between brothers and sisters is not allowed, and we know that God does not contradict Himself. There was a span of time during which intermarriage was allowed, and even Abraham married his half sister. The farther away we get from the time of creation, the more chances there are for genetic mutations and abnormalities. So, from our twenty-first century thinking, no, siblings cannot and should not marry, but when the first man and woman were created, their offspring had to marry each other in order to populate the earth.

Everyone originates from Adam and Eve, and then there was also Noah and the flood. We are all related through this bloodline as well. The flood wiped mankind from the earth with the exception of Noah and his family. Noah had three sons, Ham, Shem, and Japheth. The descendents of the Hamites are the people in the Ethiopia, Egypt region. The Europeans are descendents of Japheth, and the Shemites or Semitic people are in the Middle East.

What does "Foursquare Church" mean?

There are many Protestant denominations such as Baptist, Methodist, Church of God in Christ, etc. Our local church body is a member of the Foursquare denomination. Foursquare means

Jesus Christ is the Savior, the Healer, the Baptizer in the Holy Spirit, and the soon coming King.

Please explain Proverbs 3:5-6. I have a hard time trusting God.

It says, "Trust in the Lord with all your heart and lean not on your own understanding. In all your ways acknowledge him, and he will direct your paths." You say it's a challenge to trust God? Then you have not yet developed in your faith.

The Bible says faith comes by hearing the Word of God, so you have to get into the Word. Hebrews 11:6 says, "Without faith it is impossible to please God, because anyone who comes to him must believe that he exists and that he rewards those who earnestly seek him." You must first believe that God actually *is* and that He exists and cares for you. If you truly believe He cares for you, you will trust Him.

God is not flaky in His love for you. God does not condemn you, lie to you, or play with your emotions. God is not like the men and women we have known in our lives. He will not abandon us or lead us astray. He is perfect in His love for us. When we are facing the trials of life, trusting Him is demonstrated in our coming before His throne and saying, "God, I don't know how You are going to do this, but I trust You. I know that You love me, and I know that You are trustworthy. Please help me to trust You more!"

Trust is often proven over a duration of time. Trusting God is trusting Him when the answer isn't on the horizon, and you don't see the resolution coming. It's accepting the unknown, knowing that God is absolutely in control and has your best interest in mind. Trust is that deep rooted knowing that your heavenly father is looking out for you. Trust is not knowing the *how* of how *will things work* out, or the *what* of *what will happen next*, or even the *when* of *when will things turn around*. *Trust is knowing that God will... God will take care of me. God knows my situation. I belong to Him, and He is for me.* It's saying, "God, I trust You with my life – no matter what."

Continue to stay in the Word and build up your faith.

Put this in your perspective: If God could speak the worlds into existence out of nothing, He is able to take care of you, his beloved child.

Where did Jesus go after he was crucified until he rose again? Did he go to hell? What did he do there?

1 Peter 3:18-20 states, "For Christ also suffered once for sins, the righteous for the unrighteous, to bring you to God. He was put to death in the body but made alive in the Spirit. After being made

alive, he went and made proclamation to the imprisoned spirits – to those who were disobedient long ago when God waited patiently in the days of Noah while the ark was being built. In it only a few people, eight in all, were saved through water." There are a couple of different theological thoughts on this.

One interpretation is that Christ went to the place of the dead and preached to the spirits of those who had been alive during the time of Noah. They had rejected God and were condemned.

Another interpretation is that the spirits that he went and preached to were fallen angelic beings who had come down and mated with humankind and started a kind of hybrid race. This interpretation holds that this is the reason why God destroyed the earth in a flood. The sons of God (fallen angels), married the daughters of men (human females) and created a hyper-race that was not ordained or sanctioned by God. God destroyed them in the flood, and Jesus went and condemned those spirits which had been held in prison since that time.

What would happen if Jesus was tempted?

The Bible says that *Jesus was tempted* in every way just like you and me! In other words, he was tempted with every possible kind of temptation. Hebrews 4:15 states, "For we do not have a high priest who is unable to empathize with our weaknesses, but we have one who has been tempted in every way, just as we are – yet he did not sin.

What is your definition of heresy?

I define it the same way everyone else does: If something does not line up with Orthodox, historical, biblical Christianity, then it is heresy!

God made other planets. Scientists have discovered that some of those planets have water. Did God intend for those planets to be inhabited by human beings?

As far as we know scripturally, this is the only planet where God made His highest creation called mankind. Is there life on other planets? Could there be? Possibly, but we don't know. The Bible does not allude to those things. We know of angelic beings; we know of cherubim and seraphim and other kinds of created hosts of heaven. But as to whether life actually exists on other planets, we simply do not know. God chose to keep silent on the subject.

Who is righteous and how would you know if you are?

You are made righteous by the blood of Jesus Christ – by faith in the Lord Jesus Christ. Because of Jesus, you are in right standing with God. Romans 5:19 says, "...through the obedience of one man the many will be made righteous." You have come to the righteous One – and through him alone, you are made clean. From there you begin to live right for the Lord.

Right living produces good fruit. You are not made righteous by the works you do. You are not made righteous by saying certain prayers over and over or by attending church or serving on the usher board or by singing in the choir. You are made righteous one way and one way only: by the blood of our Lord Jesus. Good works do not produce righteousness. That's backwards. Righteousness produces good works.

The more you try to *attain righteousness* by doing good deeds, the more confused you will become. How many good deeds will make you righteous before God? What amount of good deeds would earn you entry into heaven? On the other hand, how much sin makes you unworthy? If good deeds could get you into heaven, what amount of sin would keep you out? How many good deeds would you need to override the sins in your life? It becomes a numbers game. Your good deeds would have to outweigh the bad. Imagine living in such uncertainty. You would be driven to doing good works, not out of a heart of compassion and love but to obtain points to get into heaven! The focus of your life becomes yourself and your deeds, not the Creator. Just how many points would it take to earn eternal life with God? You could never win.

You cannot cleanse yourself from your own unrighteousness. You cannot get yourself into heaven. You can do a million good deeds, but unless you recognize that you are a sinner, unworthy, and undeserving – unless you recognize that you need a Savior, you remain forever lost, worthy only to be cast out of heaven for all eternity. What could possibly cleanse you from your unrighteousness? Thank God for Jesus!

If you want to be righteous, recognize the cleansing power of the blood of Christ. Confess your sins and accept him as Savior. As you turn your life over to him, and as you allow God's Spirit to take control of your life, you begin to perform good works out of a heart of love for Christ, not out of thinking you have to get "good enough" to get into heaven and not in an effort to earn points in paradise. Please read 1 Corinthians 1:26 -31.

You are made righteous by Christ and by Christ alone. He is our righteousness.

Pastor, I want to go to heaven when I die. I've spent my life trying to be good and always fail. I know I cannot save myself, what do I do?

My friend, you are right. You cannot save yourself, and on your own, you will never be good enough. The good news is that God is waiting for you. He sent His Son Jesus to die for your sins, and He's been waiting for this moment with His arms outstretched to welcome you to Himself.

Do you recognize that you are a sinner in need of a Savior?

Are you ready to repent of your sins?

Are you ready to surrender to Jesus?

Romans 10:9 says, "If you declare with your mouth, 'Jesus is Lord,' and believe in your heart that God raised him from the dead, you will be saved." It's not a matter of saying a prayer and suddenly you have a ticket to heaven. It is recognition of one's own wickedness. It's accepting, believing, and declaring that Jesus Christ, the Son of God, is Lord.

If you believe this, simply talk to God and tell Him. Confess that you are a sinner and tell God what is in your heart. He's listening. Ask for His forgiveness. Ask Jesus to be Lord of your life.

If you have prayed this prayer to accept Jesus, please let us know. We would love to hear from you. Feel free to contact us via our website: www.faith-fellowship.us.

Do you have a question for Pastor Gary? Send your questions to askthepastor.faithfellowship@gmail.com .

About the Authors

Gary Mortara is pastor of Faith Fellowship Foursquare Church in San Leandro, California. He is the author of *Be A Man, The Beauty of A Woman,* and *Let's Get the Gay Thing Straight.*

Noted Bible teacher and popular conference speaker, Pastor Gary consistently shares the reality of Scripture with unflinching honesty, a sprinkling of humor, and large doses of love. His *I Speak Life* television and radio programs are popular broadcasts that have impacted innumerable lives.

Pastor Gary and his wife Tisha have three children and one grandchild.

Shea Gregory is a writer and speaker living in California. Shea combines performing arts and the Word to create power-packed messages that bring home the truth of the Gospel. Her writing has been featured in *Today's Christian Woman Magazine* and other private publications. Shea currently works in the education field, inspiring children and adults to fall in love with learning... and with Jesus.

Made in the USA
Columbia, SC
17 August 2023

21677106R00153